Legal Almanac Series No. 70

LEGAL REGULATION
OF
CONSUMER CREDIT

by **Stanley Morganstern, B.S., J.D.**
Member of the Ohio Bar

1972 OCEANA PUBLICATIONS, INC.
Dobbs Ferry, New York

This is the seventieth number in a series of LEGAL ALMANACS which bring you the law on various subjects in nontechnical language. These books do not take the place of your attorney's advice, but they can introduce you to your legal rights and responsibilities.

Library of Congress Cataloging in Publication Data

Morganstern, Stanley, 1941-
    Legal regulation of consumer credit.

    (Legal almanac series, no. 70)
    1. Consumer credit--Law and legislation--United
States.   I.   Title.
KF1040.Z9M67   346'.73'073   72-4364
ISBN 0-379-11083-0

Manufactured in the United States of America

TABLE OF CONTENTS

APPENDICES (cont'd)

INTRODUCTION

Credit, in its various forms, has become the mainstay of our economy. Very few persons can afford to make purchases of any substantial nature without the aid of time payments or other types of credit extension. For those persons who can adequately handle credit problems by budgeting payments against earnings, the easy availability of credit has been a blessing. For those persons who find that each month presents a panic situation as to how to meet those credit payments, the record-breaking pace at which credit has been extended has caused untolled anguish.

Time Magazine, January, 1971, uniquely characterized the payment policies of the average credit buyer as a "hat trick." That is, the debtor tosses all his bills into a hat and at the end of each month, pulls out a random few for payment. The remaining bills are left to the next month with the thought that somehow they will be paid.

The inability of the credit buyer to perform his monthly obligations has resulted in a substantial increase in the number of personal bankruptcies, trusteeships, and other insolvency proceedings. Collection agencies have been reporting a record volume of business, but unfortunately, no proportionate increase in actual collections. Likewise, credit card firms have found that their ability to collect outstanding accounts has declined significantly.

These problems are not, however, totally of the credit buyers' own making. Credit card distributors have, with no degree of selectiveness, flooded the consumer market with tickets to financial disaster. Now, in the face of rising account delinquencies, credit extenders have begun to screen credit applications more closely in an effort to cut down their losses.

The credit problem is not limited to the small credit purchaser. Businesses, large and small, have for years experienced a growing accounts receivable position not only from ultimate consumers but from other businesses. It has become customary, if not acceptable, to work with someone else's money. Each company tries to delay making payments for services and merchandise as long as possible so as to maximize its cash position and to avoid the necessity of having to pay interest on borrowed funds. This now entrenched business practice can be called "involuntary financing." Many a small business which relied upon a quick turnover of inventory suddenly found that the inventory was, in fact, turning over quickly, but that it was turning into accounts receivable rather than cash. Result: end of business.

To combat this situation, many companies are now charging interest on all payments which are not made in quick fashion. Without the added incentive for businesses to pay their suppliers on time, "involuntary financing" would continue to a point of no return.

State and Federal legislators have recognized the tremendous problems which have developed as a result of the wide use of credit both on the consumer level and among businesses. There is currently Federal legislation, the Consumer Credit Code, and many individual state statutes which have been enacted to protect the consumer in his credit purchases and in the borrowing of money. These statutes are designed to make the debtor aware of the costs of credit before he obligates himself. The acts also protect the debtor from abusive collection tactics. Garnishments are severely regulated as is the use and distribution of credit reports.

These acts are mainly disclosure types of legislation in that they require the potential creditor to inform the potential debtor of all the cost elements of any transaction. The Consumer Credit Protection Act has been characterized as the most controversial and far-reaching consumer credit law enacted in many years. Its stated purpose is:

> . . . to assure that every customer who has need for credit is given meaningful information with respect to the cost of that credit which in most cases, must be expressed in the dollar amount of finance charges, and as annual percentage rate computed on the unpaid balance of the amount financed. Other relevant credit information must also be disclosed so that the customer may readily compare the various credit terms available to him from

different sources and avoid the uniformed use of credit. 15 U.S.C.A. 1601.

Whether or not the Consumer Credit Protection Act, commonly referred to as Truth-in-Lending, will accomplish its stated purpose is open to debate. Surely reputable creditors will comply, if for no other reason than the possibility of incurring civil and criminal penalties. On the other hand, consumers must be made aware of the bare essentials of the law before it can have significant meaning to them.

Recently, this writer empaneled a jury in a case involving the Truth-in-Lending law. Only one of the fifteen prospective jurors had heard of the law and even he knew nothing of its provisions. Obviously, then, those persons would not know if the creditors they deal with were complying with the Act, and it is a safe assumption that the majority of consumers are no more informed.

The Uniform Commercial Credit Code is proposed state legislation, and in most respects, is substantially similar to the Consumer Credit Protection Act. It has been adopted in whole or in part in Colorado, Idaho, Indiana, Oklahoma, Utah, and Wyoming.

Traditionally, individual states have had small loan acts and statutes regulating the rate of interest that can be charged to individuals. These will be examined in terms of their purpose and general provisions.

It is the intent and purpose of this Almanac to examine the new as well as the traditional legislation as it pertains to our credit-minded economy.

Chapter I

CREDIT AND CONTRACTS

Identifying Credit Transactions

There are numerous types of credit transactions. Consumer credit may be divided into open end (open charge credit) and installment credit. These classifications can apply to either goods or services. There is, of course, cash credit where the debtor obtains funds upon his secured or unsecured promise to repay. This type of transaction may require a single repayment or may afford the borrower installment repayments.

Business or commercial credit usually takes the form of long-term or short-term borrowing. There may only be considerations of interest rates or there may be the very complicated consideration of state and Federal securities laws, as would be the case in the issuance of bonds and debentures. While this Almanac is concerned primarily with the regulation of private or consumer credit, there will be mention and explanation of the differences in regulation of the two basic types of credit transactions.

An open end account is one where the consumer is allowed to make any number of purchases provided the total dollar volume of his purchases does not exceed the limits established by the creditor. There is usually no written contract in this type of arrangement, and is epitomized by the normal charge account situation.

A fast growing type of credit plan is the revolving account. This arrangement falls somewhere between a true installment transaction and the open end account described above. Typically, this type of credit involves no security as is usually the case in an installment purchase where the seller retains an interest in the goods sold. A revolving account usually gives the buyer a specified line of credit. He receives a bill each month which re-

1

flects the total amount of his purchases; but unlike the open end account, the purchaser need not pay his total monthly bill, as installments are extended to him at a predetermined interest rate. There is no finance charge if the total bill is paid during the first billing period. This plan, then, gives the purchaser the option of having his account treated as either open end or an installment account without the necessity of giving security.

Installment buying is the typical credit transaction used when the item purchased is a durable good. Appliances, automobiles and large household items are traditionally bought on installment plans. Under the present state of the Federal law, finance charges and the like must be disclosed to the purchaser before the transaction is consummated. Likewise, there is considerable legislation which governs how the creditor must take and record his security interest in the goods sold. The chattel mortgage or a security agreement are the prime documents used in this type of transaction. The debtor gives a security interest in the goods he buys to either the original seller or the financial institution which extends the credit for the purchase.

The goods sold in this type of transaction can be described as those which can be repossessed. A seller would like to know that if the debtor defaults on his payments, he can reclaim the goods and resell them to mitigate his loss. There are strict statutory requirements which the creditor must follow before he will be allowed to proceed against a debtor for any deficiency which might exist after repossession and resale of the goods. These requirements will be fully discussed in another chapter but basically pertain to the giving of notice to the debtor.

Once a credit transaction can be categorized, it is then important to understand the very basic legal rights and obligations each of the parties acquires by reason of the transaction.

Contracts Establish Legal Relationships

The debtor-creditor relationship, of course, arises out of the legal relation known as contract. Even the simplest consumer transaction of necessity involves a contractual relation.

The restatement of contracts defines a contract as "a promise or set of promises for the breach of which the law gives a remedy, or the performance of which the law in some way recognizes as a duty."

Contracts can be express or implied, but we are only concerned here with those contracts which are made expressly between the parties who eventually become debtor and creditor. Each party to the contract must have legal capacity to enter into the contract. The parties must not be infants or under some judicial determination of incompetency.

There must, of course, be consideration for the promises made or the goods or services exchanged. The exchange of promises may be sufficient to satisfy that element of a valid contract; but in the debtor-creditor relationship which we are here considering, the loan of money, or the performance of services, or the delivery of goods represents the consideration for a promise to pay.

Each valid contract begins with an offer and an acceptance of that offer. Once that has been accomplished, the parties may reduce their understanding to a written agreement, or the contract may remain an oral one. In the type of relationship which we are most concerned with here, the contract is usually written. In addition to the agreement, there normally are other documents executed as part of the transaction.

If the transaction involves the giving of security of some type, either real or personal property, the debtor will be required to sign a mortgage, security agreement, financing statement, or other instrument to satisfy the various state statutes so as to give the creditor a binding interest in the property secured.

Without examining the elements of a valid contract extensively and all the problems that can arise in the construction and interpretation of contracts, it is sufficient at this point to be aware that the debtor-creditor relationship begins with a contract and that the rights and obligations of the parties are, in the first instance, governed by the terms of the contract.

The Uniform Commercial Code, in some instances, varies the traditional contract law. For instance, under common law, an offer made for a stated time could be withdrawn at any time. Under the Uniform Commercial Code, an offer made by a merchant to be held open up to three months is not revocable. Traditionally, an acceptance of an offer had to be unconditional, but under the Uniform Commercial Code there are instances where

3

the acceptance can be effective even though requiring assent by the offeror to additional terms or conditions.

A contract must be definite and agreed to in all its terms and conditions by each party to the contract. There are cases under the Code which allow a certain degree of indefiniteness, such as output and requirement contracts. These contracts are valid and enforceable under the Code.

Consideration, as previously mentioned, must be present in every contract. Under the Code, however, there need not be consideration for an agreement modifying a sales contract.

After the covenants and conditions of the contract are considered, to determine the rights and obligations of each of the parties, attention must then be directed to the laws and judicial decisions which govern the interpretation of the contract and sets forth rights and obligations not expressly contained in the contract.

In many instances the law, state or Federal, controls the course of conduct of the parties before the contract is entered into as well as conduct after there has been a breach of the contract by one of the parties. The Consumer Credit Protection Act, for example, controls the activities of potential creditors before the transaction is consummated, while the Uniform Commercial Code may control the formalities of the transaction as well as the rights of both the debtor and creditor after there has been a default of performance by either of the parties.

This Almanac will examine those statutes which control consumer credit transactions from the standpoint of formality of contract, terms of contract, enforcibility of remedies and disclosures.

Chapter II

TRUTH IN LENDING

Background

On July 1, 1969, the Consumer Credit Protection Act went into effect. This Act, designed to protect the credit buyer in all phases of his credit life, was enacted into law by the Congress of the United States.

Perhaps the best explanation of why the Act was passed and why Congress considered the legislation a must is set forth in the Act itself:

> The Congress finds that economic stabilization would be enhanced in the competition among the various financial institutions, and other firms engaged in the extension of consumer credit would be strengthened by the informed use of credit.

> The informed use of credit results from the awareness of the cost thereof by consumers. It is the purpose of this title to assure a meaningful disclosure of credit terms so that the consumer will be able to compare more readily the various terms available to him and avoid the uninformed use of credit.

The Consumer Credit Protection Act includes three subchapters. The first subchapter has come to be known as truth-in-lending and primarily covers the disclosures which must be made to a customer, potential credit buyer or borrower before, or at the time credit is extended to him. The second subchapter of the Act pertains to restrictions on garnishments, and the third deals with credit reporting agencies.

5

General Provisions

Since the purpose of the Act is to control consumer credit, there are certain transactions involving credit which are exempt from the operation of the Act. For example, credit given
or used in business, or commercial or governmental use need
not follow the same procedures of disclosure that are required
in consumer transactions. Likewise, security and commodity
transactions are exempt. An extension of credit in the amount of
more than $25,000, except as to real estate transactions, is ex-
empt from the disclosure provisions of the Act as are transactions
under public utilities tariffs filed with the state and Federal power commissions. These actions which are regulated by the states
are exempt.

Basically, the Act extends its coverage to all persons who
in the course of their business regularly extend or arrange for
consumer credit. Consequently, a casual extension of credit
would not be subject to the provisions of the Act. The act does,
however, cover those persons who offer to extend or arrange for
the extension of consumer credit. Therefore, a real estate broker
who does not in his business extend credit but regularly offers to
arrange for the extension of credit with a local financial institution would be subject to the pain and penalties of the Act if proper
disclosures were not made.

Since coverage under the Consumer Credit Protection Act
does not extend to the casual or infrequent extension or arrangement of credit, the small businessman who occasionally extends
credit to his customers may not be subject to the Federal legislation. On the other hand, if the small businessman normally extends credit as a part of his business, he will be bound by the
provisions of the Act. As a general rule, banks, savings and
loan associations, credit card issuers, auto dealers, credit un-
ions, consumer finance companies, craftsmen and the like, are
covered within the scope of the Act.

Installment payments made to a person in the position of
a bailor are not within the scope of the Act. Likewise, lease
arrangements are not covered so long as the arrangement is not
merely a disguised sale. If the lessee is to pay an amount over
the term of the lease which substantially approximates the value
of the property leased, and the lessee is eventually to become

the owner of the property, there is a good chance that the transaction will be treated as a sale and be subject to the disclosure provisions of the Act.

While it might appear that securities transactions involving margin buying where interest is charged should be covered by the Act, the Securities Exchange Commission has exclusive control of these transactions. Thus the Consumer Credit Protection Act would not apply. The same is true of any other area of transactions governed by other Federal legislation.

The Federal Reserve Board, which provides the rules and regulations for application of the Act, may exempt individual states from coverage under the Act if those States have enacted legislation substantially similar to the Federal law. Those statutes may be more restrictive but may not be less restrictive than the Federal Act. Inconsistent state laws which require fewer disclosures different in form, substance, terminology or time of delivery will not be effective as against the Federal Act. But the Federal Act does not nullify state laws to the extent those laws do not clash with the Federal Act.

An important aspect of the Act is that it in no way affects the validity of any transaction. With the exception of the recission provisions of the Act, a consumer cannot expect to be relieved of his obligations under a contract merely because the creditor failed to comply with some provision of the Consumer Credit Protection Act. Nothing in the Act, including the civil and criminal penalties provided therein, affect the substantive aspects of the sale or loan.

The Federal Reserve Board is basically charged with prescribing regulations necessary to carry out the purposes of the disclosure subchapter of the Act. The first of these regulations is known as Regulation Z, by which name the Act is often called. Other provisions of the Act may involve enforcement by such diverse agencies as the Civil Aeronautics Board, Federal Trade Commission, Federal Housing Administration, Veterans Administration, Department of Housing and the Secretary of Labor.

Definitions

Definitions are important in understanding the provisions of this Act as is true in all statutory enactments. "Consumer credit" is that credit offered or extended to a natural person upon which a finance charge may be imposed. Again this is limited to a personal family or consumer type transaction as opposed to a business or agricultural purpose.

There may be certain situations in which a finance charge or interest is not incurred, but the transaction may still fall within the scope of the Consumer Protection Act. If the repayment of the loan or credit requires more than four installments, the transaction is covered by the Act no matter that no interest or other charges for credit are made.

"Credit" as defined by the Act, is that right granted by a creditor to a debtor to defer payment of a debt or to incur a debt and defer its payment.

A "creditor" is a person or organization who regularly extends credit or arranges for the extension of credit for which payment of a finance charge is required. Someone arranges for the extension of credit when he provides or offers to provide the consumer with credit to be extended by someone other than himself. This is especially true when the person arranging the credit is to receive some kind of compensation or fee. It is not necessary that there be such a monetary arrangement if the person making the arrangement for credit has knowledge of the credit terms and, in fact, participates in the preparation of the necessary documents, or contracts to consummate the transaction.

Perhaps the most important definitions contained in the Act for disclosure purposes are "amount financed," "annual percentage rate," and the "finance charge."

The "amount financed" means that amount of credit which the consumer will actually have. The "finance charge" includes interest, points, carrying charges, loan fees, finders fees, investigation of credit report fees, charges for insurance written in connection with the credit transaction and any other change including the cost paid by the consumer to the creditor for discounting of the paper.

Items such as filing fees, license fees, and taxes required to be paid by law are excluded from the finance charge even though they were paid over a deferred period of time.

Insurance premiums may also be excluded from the finance charge if the insurance is a substitute for a security interest, rather than the type of insurance normally written in connection with credit transactions.

Also excluded from the finance charge are such charges as late payments, costs and all default or delinquency charges. Those charges in connection with real estate transactions, such as title insurance premiums, survey charges, title examination charges, fees for preparation of documents including deeds and mortgages, amounts required to be paid into escrow in proration of taxes, insurance, rents and the like, notary fees, appraisal fees and the credit report charges, are not to be included in the finance charge.

An equally important definition contained in the statute is the "annual percentage rate." That is, the annual per cent rate of finance charge as determined in accordance with the provisions of the statute. It is the basis for the cost of the credit and it is the basis on which the consumer is to shop for his credit. The Consumer Credit Protection Act contemplates that the consumer will use the annual percentage rate as a basis for comparing the cost of credit before making a decision as to which of several credit extensions he will accept.

The computation of the annual percentage rate is on its face quite complicated but is made easier by the Federal Reserve Board which supplies tables for such computation. The annual percentage rate may vary in accordance with the kind of credit being extended. That is, open end credit accounts, revolving accounts, charge accounts and the like result in different annual percentage rates than when they are computed in credit transactions other than open end accounts.

Other definitions that are necessary for an understanding of the Act are set forth below.

> 1. advertisement - any commercial message in any newspaper, magazine, leaflet, flyer, or catalog, on radio, television, or public address system, in direct mail literature or other printed material, on any interior or exterior sign or display, in any window display, in any point of transaction literature or pricetag which is delivered or made available to a customer or prospective customer in any manner whatsoever.

2. cash price - the price at which the creditor offers in the ordinary course of business, to sell for cash the property or services which are the subject of a consumer credit transaction.

The above definition of cash price may include the cash price of accessories related to the sale, such as delivery, installation, alterations, modification and improvements and may include taxes to the extent imposed on the cash sale. The cash price does not, however, include any other charges that would be of the type to be included in the amount financed.

3. credit sale - any sale with respect to which consumer credit is extended or arranged by the seller. The term includes any contract in the form of a bailment or lease if the bailee or leassee contracts to pay as compensation for use a sum substantially equivalent to or in excess of the aggregate value of the property and services involved...

Annual Percentage Rate

That annual percentage rate which we have previously defined can vary depending upon how it is calculated. Proper application of the annual percentage rate requires different calculation depending upon the type of credit extended. Open-end transactions require a different mentod of computation of the annual percentage rate than do closed-end transactions.

It is interesting to note that almost every computation of an annual percentage rate will result in a rate higher than that allowed to be charged under state usury laws. The usury laws normally apply to face amount of interest while an annual percentage rate reflects not only an effective rate of interest, but includes all costs of credit in addition to just bare interest.

A revolving account is, of course, a form of open-end credit. The annual percentage rate for such accounts can be computed in one of several ways. It can be based on the application of periodic rates, on a fixed or minimum charge, or on a range of balances. In other words, it can be based on a fixed rate for a fixed period, on a fixed or minimum rate for no definite period, or a fixed rate depending upon the bracket in which the principal balance falls.

The periodic rate method requires that the periodic rate be multiplied by the number of periods in one year. A one-and-a-half percent monthly interest charge on a given balance would result in an annual percentage rate of 18 per cent. If, however, there are two or more periodic rates, the annual percentage rate can be computed by either stating each as an annual rate or combining them as a single rate. If the latter method is chosen, the total finance charge is divided by the sum of the balances to which it applies. The quotient obtained therefrom is then multiplied by the number of billing cycles in a single year.

When the finance charge is based on a minimum or fixed rate that in no way is affected by the periodic rate, the annual percentage rate is found by dividing the total finance charge by the amount of the balance to which the charge applies. That quotient is then multiplied by the number of billing cycles in a year. This procedure is valid where the fixed or minimum charge exceeds fifty cents for a monthly or longer period, but where the charge is less than fifty cents for such a period, a different computation is required. In such cases, the annual percentage rate is found by multiplying each periodic rate by the number of periods in a year no matter any minimum or fixed charge. A fifty cent charge on a balance of $33 results in an annual percentage rate of approximately one-and-one half per cent.

When the finance charge expressed as an annual percentage rate is based on the range of principal balances over the billing period, the finance charge is divided by the median of the range of balances and the result multiplied by the number of periods in one year.

All of these methods of computation may result in figures not precisely correct. Recognizing this, a creditor is allowed an error of one-quarter per cent in his computation. If an error of greater magnitude occurs, the creditor may still save himself from liability by disclosing the correction to the consumer within the time limits specified in the statute itself and the Board Regulations.

Closed-end credit requires the use of either the actuarial method or the application of the United States Rule in computing the annual percentage rate.

11

The United States Rule dictates that the finance charge be computed on the declining unpaid balance for the actual length of time that balance remains unpaid. When a payment is made, it is first applied to unpaid finance charges and then to principal. If any one payment exceeds the unpaid finance charge, the excess is applied to the principal balance. Subsequent payments are applied in the same manner until the principal balance reaches zero.

As in the case of open-end transactions, the precise calculation of the annual percentage rate on closed-end transactions depends upon the particular credit arrangements. The transaction might be a straight installment plan. The terms might require a single advance by the creditor with equal payments to be made at either uniform or nonuniform intervals. Payments may be due in unequal amounts at stated or variable intervals. Credit terms may involve a single advance by the creditor and a single payment by the debtor or multiple advances by the creditor with varying repayment plans. Some arrangements may require the debtor to maintain deposits with the creditor to secure repayment.

Since there may be so wide a variation in the precise terms of the credit extended, the Federal Reserve Board has been empowered to prescribe alternate methods of computation that would provide simplicity and reasonably accurate results. One such method is the constant ratio method, permissible under Regulation Z, for use in closed-end transactions.

What could be simpler than $R = 2PC - A (N+1)$? In that formula, R is the annual percentage rate, P is the number of payment periods, C is the finance charge, A is the principal balance, and N is the number of installments to be made.

Another factor which may vary the annual percentage rate is whether or not the loan is discounted in advance. A borrower who repays a \$100 loan at 6% add-on interest, actually repays \$106. The annual percentage rate is 11%, assuming a one-year period since the borrower only had the full use of the \$100 until his first payment. Assuming the same facts, a borrower would pay at an 11 1/2% rate if the loan is discounted in advance. The borrower only receives \$94 and must repay \$100.

In an effort to make the computation of the annual percentage rate as simple as possible, the Federal Reserve Board has published volumes of charts. These publications provide not only quick computation help, but also instructions on how to use the charts. They may be obtained either from a local Federal Reserve Bank or from the Board of Governors of the Federal Reserve System, Washington, D.C. 20551.

Disclosures

The Truth-in-Lending Act provides for disclosures to be made by the creditor or one who arranges the credit transaction prior to the actual extension of credit. The information may be disclosed to the consumer in the contract, on the document of indebtedness signed by the purchaser, or in a separate instrument.

Typical disclosure requirements are those on a consumer credit sale as opposed to an open account or revolving charge account. The creditor must disclose the following items:

1. The cash price of the property or services purchased.

2. The amount of any downpayment, including the value assigned to a trade-in.

3. The difference between the cash price and the down-payment or value of the trade-in.

4. All other charges itemized individually which, although not part of the finance charge, are included in the amount of the credit extended.

5. The total amount to be financed (This would be the difference between the cash price and the downpayment, plus all other charges similarly included but not part of the finance charge.)

6. The amount of the finance charge. (This need not be shown in the case of a sale of a dwelling, but in all other transactions, it must be shown. It also must be designated as a time-price differential or some other term which would be appli-

cable. Most finance companies and the like have chosen to use the actual words "finance charge" so that there is no question but the item is included on the disclosure statement.)

7. The finance charge must then be expressed as an "annual percentage rate" except in those cases where the finance charge does not exceed $5, and the amount financed does not exceed $75, or where the finance charge does not exceed $7.50 and the amount financed for that charge is $75 or less.

8. The number, amount and due dates or periods of payments scheduled to repay the indebtedness must be set forth.

9. If there is a default charge, late charge or delinquency charge, it must be set forth.

10. If the creditor is acquiring a security interest in any property as a result of the sale or in connection with the extension of credit, that property must be clearly identified.

Since the disclosures are normally given by people who may be unfamiliar with the precise calculations of the annual percentage rates and since there might be minute changes in the amounts shown on the disclosure statements, the Act provides correction procedures. A creditor can relieve himself of liability if within fifteen days after discovering an error made on the disclosure statement and prior to any action taken by the consumer to enforce his rights by judicial process, he issues a corrected statement. The creditor may notify the consumer of the error so long as he makes the proper adjustments and does not require the consumer to pay a finance charge which would be greater than the amount or the percentage rate actually disclosed to the consumer by the original disclosure papers. If a creditor inadvertently makes an error and the consumer brings an action, the creditor may likewise avoid any liability in that situation if he can show by a preponderance of the evidence, the greater weight of the evidence, that the violation was not intentional. He must further show that there was a bona fide error and that the procedures he maintains for the disclosure of such information would reasonably avoid such errors.

If, however, the creditor fails to disclose information or discloses such information in a manner which cannot be justified as being unintentional or an inadvertent error, he may be liable in a civil action. The consumer debtor may bring an action in any court, including the District Courts of the United States, and recover an amount equal to twice the amount of the finance charge made in that transaction; but the amount of his recovery may not be less than $100 or greater than $1,000. In an effort to encourage this type of action which, of necessity, involves attorneys fees and the like, the Act specifically grants to a successful plaintiff in such situations reasonable attorneys fees and the costs of the action to be paid by the defendant creditor.

In many transactions, such as the purchase of an automobile, the dealer and the institution which will eventually hold the paper, require that the consumer provide adequate evidence of property and liability insurance. If the creditor or automobile dealer arranges for the issuance of such insurance and includes the premiums thereof as part of the transaction, those charges must be included in the finance charge. In the absence of such arrangement, the creditor must, in clear and specific language as part of the written disclosures, tell the consumer debtor either that he may choose the person through whom the insurance is to be obtained or if obtained, from or through the creditor, the cost of the insurance.

Likewise, charges or premiums for life, accident or health insurance premiums must be included in the finance charge unless such insurance is not a factor in the approval of the credit. If insurance is not required to complete the extension of credit, that fact must be clearly disclosed in writing to the consumer. Further, to exclude the costs of insurance from the finance charge, the consumer must, if he desires to obtain insurance in connection with the transaction, give "specific affirmative written indication" of his desire to do so after written disclosure is made to him of the cost of such insurance.

The particular disclosures required for each type of transaction will be discussed in connection with these transactions. Each type requires various disclosures, but generally disclosures are aimed at providing the consumer with complete information as to the total cost of credit and all its component parts, including insurance.

Rescindable Transactions

Another important consideration of the Truth-in-Lending legislation is that some transactions may be resicndable. The consumer may, within a stated period, elect to cancel the transaction. Upon making the goods available to the seller, he may cancel any obligation he may have had under the transaction. Basically, a transaction is rescindable where by the terms of the security given or by other circumstances of the loan, the creditor or seller is entitled to or may obtain a judgment lien or mortgage upon the principal place of residence of the borrower or debtor.

This situation is particularly relevant when either a second mortgage is given to secure the proceeds of the loan or where the seller takes a cognovit note. The terms of the note may entitle a creditor to a judgment without notice to the debtor, and upon obtaining such judgment, may entitle him to a judgment lien on the principal residence of the debtor. When a transaction is a rescindable one, there are additional disclosure responsibilities placed on the creditor. He must inform the debtor that the transaction is in fact rescindable, giving to the debtor the proper notice of rescission which the debtor may exercise and return to the creditor within three business days from the consummation of the transaction or the disclosure whichever is the later in time.

In order for a transaction to be rescindable, it must be one involving the extension or arrangement of consumer credit .The creditor must retain or be able to acquire a security interest or judgment lien on the principal residence of the consumer. Residence, as defined by the Act, means that real property in which a consumer resides or expects to reside. Residence includes any parcel of land on which the consumer resides or expects to reside.

The security interest or judgment lien can arise in one of several ways. It can be, as mentioned previously, a real property mortgage or judgment lien arising out of a confession of judgment on a cognovit note. There are other ways which are perhaps more subtle. These include deeds of trust, mechanics' liens, material men's liens, and artisians' liens. Also, possibilities arise in connection with vendors' liens or any other security interest granted or perfected under the Uniform Commercial Code.

Previous to the adoption of Truth-in-Lending legislation, a cognovit note was the most prevalent form of security taken. Upon default, the creditor could reduce it to judgment and it was a simple process to obtain a judgment lien on the principal place of residence of the debtor, which could then be foreclosed. Thus, the extension of credit could readily result in the loss of one's home.

Since the adoption of Truth-in-Lending legislation, many potential creditors and sellers of goods on credit have modified the traditional cognovit note to include a waiver of their rights to obtain a lien on the principal place of residence. As will be explained later, this waiver is a form of self-protection for such creditors.

The waiver of such liens does not, however, preclude the judgment creditor from obtaining a lien on any other piece of real estate owned by the consumer or creditor, but does specifically prohibit him from obtaining a judgment lien which could result in the loss of a debtor's home. The cognovit situation applies not only to the sale of goods, but may also apply to professional services rendered by doctors, lawyers, dentists, and the like who, as security for their fee, take back cognovit notes.

Disclosures and Procedure

Every seller or borrower must provide the debtor with two copies of a notice containing his right to rescind the transaction. The notice must be printed on one side of a separate statement and must identify specifically the transaction which gave rise to the debtor's right to rescind. Even the size of the print is specified by the Act and the language must be exactly as prescribed in the Act. The debtor must be informed as to the precise nature of the effect of his rescission should he decide to exercise it.

In order for the consumer or borrower to exercise his

right to rescind, he must do so in writing. Again, it must be exercised before midnight of the third business day after the right to rescind becomes effective.

Three business days may really result in more actual days depending upon the time of the week the sale is made and the occurrence of holidays. A business day is any calendar day except Sunday or the holidays of New Years, Washington's Birthday, Memorial Day, Independence Day, Labor Day, Veterans Day, Thanksgiving and Christmas. Thus if the sale takes place on a Friday, with a holiday falling on the next Monday, both Sunday and Monday would not be counted in computing the three business-day period.

The customer or consumer may mail his notice of rescission or he may telegraph it to the creditor. The effective date of mailing or telegraphing is the day on which it is sent. It is important to note that the creditor need not actually receive the notice of rescission before midnight of the third business day. The Act only requires that the notice be mailed or telegraphed before the expiration of that time. Once the consumer or borrower does exercise his right to rescind, he cannot be liable for any charges or security interest which the creditor may have been able to charge or obtain.

Upon receiving notification of the rescission, the creditor must, interestingly enough, return all moneys or properties he has received in connection with the transaction. If a security interest was perfected, the creditor must take whatever steps are necessary to terminate that interest. When the creditor does return the moneys and or properties and cancels the security interest he has obtained, then and only then, does the customer become obligated to tender the property he has received in the transaction.

At this point it seems that legislators have bent over backwards to protect the consumer or debtor. The tender of the property by the debtor may be made at his residence or any other place the property is located. This becomes very important in that if the seller or creditor does not take possession of the goods within ten days after they have been tendered by the consumer, the consumer acquires ownership of the property and has no further obligation to pay for it. Carrying this to absurdity, if one were to purchase an automobile in Texas, drive it to Maine and within

18

three business days give notice of recission, he could tender the auto by informing the seller it was located in Maine. If for some reason the seller could not arrange to take possession of that car within ten days, the consumer would acquire ownership without any obligation to pay for it. This situation may, in its application, sound absurd, but it could happen and debtors could make a practice of obtaining property without having to pay for it. This, then, is why auto dealers and other dealers of durable consumer products have waived their right to a lien on the buyer's place of residence. By so doing, the transaction is no longer rescindable and the dealer no longer faces these remote but possible situations.

There may be situations in which the debtor wishes to waive or forego his right to rescission. Normally this right is not waiverable. If, however, there is a personal financial emergency or if the customer in his own mind determines that the three-day waiting period will jeopardize his welfare, health or safety, it may be waived. Further, if the waiting period will endanger the property being acquired in the transaction, the consumer may waive such right to rescind. The Act, however, requires that before there can be a waiver of the right to rescind, the consumer must furnish the creditor with a signed statement of the reason why he requires the waiver of his right to rescind.

Exceptions

There are some important exceptions to the rescindable transaction law as stated above. Normally, any transaction which involves a lien or security interest on the principal place of residence is a rescindable transaction, except that a first mortgage (a purchase money mortgage) on a home which is to be the principal place of residence of the debtor is excepted from the application of the Act.

A first mortgage that is made for the initial construction of the debtor's principal place of residence or a loan made to satisfy the construction loan is not rescindable. Likewise, a loan which provides the debtor with permanent financing of his principal place of residence is also excepted.

A subordinate lien on a principal place of residence made subordinate sometime after its creation is exempt from application of this section if it was exempt at the time it was originally created. Any advancement made for agricultural purposes under an open-end real estate mortgage or other type of lien is also exempt. Disclosures required under the general disclosure sections of the Act had to have been made at the time the security interest was acquired by the creditor or at any time prior to the first advance made on that loan. This, of course, only applies to advances made after the effective date of the Truth-in-Lending Act.

Effectively, then, all second mortgages on a debtor's principal place of residence are rescindable transactions. In general terms, those transactions by which a debtor obtains permanent financing to either buy or build his home are not rescindable transactions. It should be noted that the rescindable transaction provisions apply only to the principal place of residence of the debtor and do not apply to vacation homes, summer cottages or the like.

Craftsmen

The rescindable transaction provisions of the Act have special significance to a contractor or subcontractor who is performing work on the principal place of residence of the debtor. Before this legislation, such craftsmen were secure in knowing that they could obtain a mechanic's lien if and when a debtor did not pay him or he was not paid for his services by the general contractor. Under the Truth-in-Lending legislation, the debtor who may find himself with a lien upon his premises must be given the proper disclosures and be made aware that the transaction is a rescindable one. The informed craftsman will now wait three days before beginning any work on the premises. Otherwise, he may find that if he begins the job immediately, he is subject to the rescission provisions of the Act and his work may have been for naught.

Conclusion

The rescission provisions of the Act have had, perhaps, the most far-reaching effects of any of the Truth-in-Lending requirements. It has changed the very basic collection practices of creditors and has added protection of a consumer's home.

Chapter III

TRANSACTIONS COVERED BY CONSUMER
CREDIT PROTECTION ACT

A.

CREDIT CARDS

The Consumer Credit Protection Act contains a portion applicable to the issuance and use of credit cards. Almost every consumer has received credit cards which he did not order, tempting him with the easy availability of goods and services. The Consumer Credit Protection Act prohibits the indiscriminate issuing of credit cards and requires that no credit card shall be issued except in response to a request for an application for that card. This does, not, however, prohibit the renewal of a credit card or the substitution for an already accepted card. This portion of the Consumer Credit Protection Act became effective October 26, 1970.

The use of credit cards has given rise to an area of insurance coverage not before widely used. Many companies have now devised a policy of insurance whereby a credit card holder will be insured against any use of his card by unauthorized persons either through theft or loss. Previous to October 26, 1970, a consumer would be responsible for charges incurred on his card until he notified the credit card company that the card had been either lost or stolen. The Act now limits the consumer's liability for unauthorized use of his card to $50, assuming that certain procedures have been followed by the credit card issuer. If these procedures have not been followed, a credit card holder will have no liability for the unauthorized use of his card.

If the card is not an accepted credit card, there is no liability on the part of the credit card user. The credit card issuer, in order to insure the fact that the consumer will be liable for the $50, must have given adequate notice to the credit card holder of that potential liability and it must have provided the card holder with a self-addressed prestamped notification to be mailed by the card holder if and when a loss or theft of the credit card occurs. If the unauthorized use takes place before the card issuer has been notified that the unauthorized use may occur, then the $50 liability may be incurred. If, however, the credit card holder notifies the issuer that the loss may occur and the loss does not, in fact, occur until after notification has been sent, then there will be no liability on the part of the credit card holder.

In addition to all these requirements, cards issued on or after the effective date of the Statute will carry no liability to the credit card holder for its unauthorized use unless the issuer has provided a method whereby the user of the card can be reasonably identified as the person authorized thereunder.

In any case where notice is to be sent by a card holder to the issuer, all the card holder need do is take those steps which are reasonably required in the ordinary course of business to provide the issuer with such information. It does not matter that any particular officer, employee or agent of the issuer in fact receives the information.

If and when a card issuer seeks to enforce liability for either the authorized use or the unauthorized use of a credit card, he has the burden of proof to show that the conditions of liability for the unauthorized use of the card as set forth above existed, and to further show that it was either an authorized or unauthorized use. If the liability of a card holder is further limited by the terms and conditions of the agreement between the consumer and the credit card issuer, or by state law, then the $50 limitation set forth in the Consumer Credit Protection Act will not apply. In other words, the most stringent restriction, either by contract, local law, or federal law as to the liability of the credit card holder, will be deemed applicable. No matter the terms of the agreement or state law, the credit card holder's liability cannot be greater than the $50 limitation established by the Act.

Most states provide that the fraudulent use or unauthorized use of a credit card constitutes a crime, usually denominated as larceny by trick. Other states have enacted specific penal provisions as to the unauthorized use of a credit card or the use

22

of a credit card which is counterfeit or fictitious. The Consumer Credit Protection Act, being federal legislation, can only provide criminal penalties when such cards are used in a manner affecting interstate or foreign commerce. The Act provides a fine of not more than $1,000 or imprisonment for not more than five years, or both for any person who uses a counterfeit, fictitious, altered, forged, lost, stolen or fraudulently obtained credit card to obtain goods and services or both, having a retail value aggregating $5,000 or more.

B.

CREDIT ADVERTISING

Advertising of credit terms has long been a source of consumer confusion. How often has one seen the ad, "$10 down, $10 a week?" This type of advertising can be misleading in that it utterly fails to disclose the price of the goods, the cost of credit, or the number of payments to be made. The Consumer Credit Protection Act attempts to curtail advertising of this nature and to insure the consumer of full disclosure of all pertinent terms. If the creditor wishes to engage in credit advertising, he must comply with the advertising provisions of the Act.

Advertising provisions of the Consumer Credit Protection Act, like the other provisions of the Act, do not apply to transactions in excess of $25,000, business or commercial dealings, credit to governments or organizations, transactions by broker-dealers registered with the securities and Exchange Commission, or to some transactions involving charges for public utility services.

Generally, the Act prohibits the advertisement of any credit terms unless full disclosure is made. The precise disclosures required depend upon the type of credit being advertised. If open-end credit is advertised, the potential creditor must fully disclose all items that he would have to disclose upon consummation of the transaction.

When an ad pertaining to open-end credit recites the percentage of finance charge, a Comparative Index of Credit Cost, or indicates downpayment or repayment terms, all of the sub-

sequent data must be disclosed.
1. Any period during which no credit charge is made.
2. Method of determining the balance on which the credit is levied.
3. Method of determining the amount of the finance charge, including any minimum or fixed amount.
4. The range of balances on which periodic rates will be imposed and the periodic rates expressed as annual percentage rates.
5. Method of computing additional charges and circumstances under which they will be imposed.

If the advertising relates to other than open-end credit, disclosures must be made as to the following items:
1. Annual percentage rate
2. Amount of the loan or cash price
3. Downpayment required, if any
4. Period of repayment
5. Number, amount and due dates of payments
6. Deferred payment price or total of the payments

Once the creditor begins credit advertising, he must fully comply with the disclosure provisions. Full disclosure of these items is meant to put the potential debtor on notice of the terms and, in effect, or at least in purpose, prevent the creditor from changing the terms before completion of the transaction. Like all advertising, credit advertising was used to bring customers into ones' place of business. More often than not, the terms advertised did not apply to the particular deal in which the customer was interested.

Imposition of credit advertising disclosure requirements has not completely prohibited creditors from advertising credit without giving full disclosure. Credit men have been advised through at least one of their industry publications that they may still make such representations as "easy credit" or "liberal credit terms available." The use of these terms does not necessitate any further disclosure of terms. This interpretation of the Act appears to be correct.

A further restriction on credit advertising is imposed by the Act. A creditor advertising that a specific amount of credit or installment payments can be arranged must be one who usually and customarily arranges or will arrange credit amounts or installments for that period and in that amount. Likewise, if the ad states that there will be no downpayment or that a specified downpayment is acceptable, the creditor must usually and customarily accept downpayments in the amount advertised.

These advertising restrictions apply to any ad which is meant to aid, promote or directly or indirectly assist any extension of credit, and apply to single-page advertisements as well as catalogs and multi-page circulations.

Under the terms of the Act, catalogs and multi-page advertisements are to be considered a single advertisement if there is contained therein a table or schedule which clearly and conspicuously makes the proper disclosures. Further, if statements of credit terms appear in places other than the table or schedule, it must refer to the page or pages on which the table or schedule appears. Each statement may, of course, disclose all of the applicable credit terms.

Liability for violation of the advertising provisions of the Consumer Credit Protection Act is limited to the creditor. Willful violations are punishable by imprisonment of up to one year and/or a $5,000 fine. Liability does not extend to the media or its agents which disseminate the ad to the general public. Coverage of the Act applies to any type of mass media advertising including television, radio, newspapers, magazines, leaflets, flyers, price tags, direct mail, window displays, billboards and even public address announcements.

Obviously, creditors whose terms are more lenient than their competitors will take full advantage of full disclosure advertising. Those creditors whose terms are not competitive will refrain from advertising or confine their announcements to very general terms.

Unlike other provisions of the Act, there is no possible exemption from the advertising provisions. Thus, states having or considering same or similar laws will not in any event be exempted from this particular application of the Consumer Credit Protection Act.

The Federal Reserve Board is authorized to interpret and provide further regulations as to the Consumer Credit Protection Act. In an opinion letter concerning advertising of credit, the

Board has recommended that when terms are advertised as to sales which will vary in total price from transaction to transaction, a hypothetical example which clearly corresponds to the most common size of that type transaction be used. The particular inquiry to the Board concerned the sale of heating and air conditioning equipment which, by necessity, would involve a different total sale price for each installation, depending upon the work required. All the credit advertiser can do in such instances if fairly set forth an example of a relatively typical transaction.

State Laws

While the Consumer Credit Protection Act requires full disclosure of all items in credit advertising, state statutes have for many years prohibited misrepresentation in credit advertising. Generally, the state statutes pertaining to credit advertising seek to prevent false or deceptive representations as to the rates, terms, or conditions for loans. Specifically, banks, consumer loan companies and other licensed lending institutions are governed by these state statutes.

<u>C.</u>

<u>REAL ESTATE TRANSACTIONS</u>

Like other consumer credit transactions, real estate transactions are covered by the Truth-in-Lending Act when such transactions are made for personal rather than business purposes. The Act covers real estate transactions including not only the extension of a mortgage, but also any type of transaction involving the obtaining of a security interest in real estate. A security interest means any interest in property which secures payment or performance of an obligation. It includes such things as a real property mortgage, deed of trust, resulting judgment liens, mechanics' liens, materialman's liens, artisans' liens, vendors' liens and an interest in a lease when used to secure payment or performance of the obligation.

A real property transaction is defined as any extension of credit in connection with which a security interest in real property is or will be obtained or acquired. Real property is defined under Regulation Z as property which under the state law in which it is located, would be considered real property.

It has previously been mentioned that any transaction involving a total amount to be financed in excess of $25,000 is exempt from operation of the Truth-in-Lending Act. However, real estate transactions, no matter the amount, are covered. The $25,000 maximum does not apply.

It is important in real estate transactions to remember the definition of a creditor, which includes not only the person or lending institution which actually extends the credit but one who regularly extends or arranges for the extension of credit. Thus, in a normal real estate transaction, real estate brokers, mortgage brokers and any other person who takes an active role in arranging the financing would be covered by the Act. The general exemption for one who extends or arranges for the extension of credit on a one-time basis applies in real estate transactions. Thus if an individual sells his residence and arranges for financing for the buyer, he would not be covered by the Act, as this would be a casual extension of credit or casual arrangement for the extension of credit. If he takes back a second mortgage as part of the transaction and does not regularly do this as a business, then that transaction would be exempt from application of the Act.

Likewise, the real estate transaction is exempt if it is made for the benefit of a contractor or builder within the scope of his business. A construction loan made to a builder or contractor, whose primary purpose is to sell the building at its completion for a profit, would not be covered by the Act.

Like all statutory enactments, there is tremendous room for interpretation. If an individual were to obtain financing to pruchase an apartment building in which he was not going to live, there would be no question that the loan was for business purposes and not covered by the Act. But consider the situation where an individual buys an apartment with a few suites and intends to live in one of the suites. The question, then, is whether or not this loan was primarily for personal family household purposes and thus covered by the Act. If, of course, it were a twenty-five suite apartment and he were only occupying one suite, then it could readily be seen that it would be a business purpose. But if the apartment contained only a few units, then whether or not it is covered by the Act becomes questionable and subject to judicial interpretation.

A real estate transaction falls within the category of other than open-end credit. In other words, it is not a charge account, revolving account or the like, and is subject to the disclosure provisions of the Act pertaining to other than open-end credit transactions. Disclosures must, of course, be made prior to the consummation of a transaction so that the declaration of purpose of the Act may be fulfilled. That is, the consumer or borrower should be made aware of the cost of credit prior to the consummation of the transaction so that he may "shop for credit." When is a transaction consummated? This is a rather difficult question which is subject to extensive judicial interpretation. If a consumer is given a written commitment for a loan, is that transaction consummated at the time the commitment is given, or at the time the actual documents are executed? These questions have not yet been answered.

Disclosures

Disclosures which must be given in other than open-end credit transactions are set forth specifically in the statute. Disclosures once again must be made prior to the consummation of the transaction, and the consumer must be provided with a duplicate of the instrument or statement by which the required disclosures are made. Disclosures can be made on the instrument evidencing the indebtedness or on a separate document. The information which must be disclosed includes the date on which the finance charge begins to accrue, the finance charge expressed as an annual percentage rate, the number, amount and due dates or periods of payment, the method of computing the amount of any default, delinquency or similar late charge payments, the description or identification of security, description of any penalty charge that may be imposed by the seller or his assignee for prepayment, identification and method of computing the unearned portion of the finance charge in the event of prepayment, the amount of credit, prepaid finance charges and required deposit balances, and except in a case of a loan secured by a first lien or equivalent security interest on a dwelling made to finance the purchase of that dwelling, the total amount of the finance charge with a description of each amount included therein with the specific use of the term finance charge.

Finance charge must be expressed as an annual percentage rate except where the finance charge does not exceed $5 on an amount not exceeding $75 or where the finance charge does not exceed $7.50 on an amount financed not exceeding $75.

With the exception of purchase-money first mortgages, the creditor must disclose the total dollar amount of the interest over the entire life of the loan. This amount can, of course, be staggering, and the home buyer might think twice about purchasing a home if he really knew what it cost him. On the other hand, the disclosure of the annual percentage rate presents no great problem or deterrent to the home buyer who usually can't or doesn't interpolate that to a dollar figure. If the purchaser of a $25,000 home realized that that amount of mortgage money at six and three-quarters per cent over a twenty-five year life of the mortgage will cost him $26,819 in interest, he just might be hesitant about consummating the transaction.

Congress did not want to discourage the consumer from purchasing a home, and it is reasonable to assume that they did not want unduly to incur the wrath of our banking institutions; hence, the first mortgage exemption. To the contrary, however, Congress was very concerned with transactions which result in second mortgages on the homes of sometimes unsuspecting home owners. These second mortgages often arise from home improvement transactions or from direct loans when the consumer was in dire need of money. In more cases than not, the consumer did not know the cost of financing the home improvement or the cost of the loan. Often the home improvement salesman had the consumer sign a stack of documents which, unknown to the consumer contained a mortgage form.

Hopefully the Truth-in-Lending law will at least discourage this type of practice. The law requires that the mortgage disclose the interest rate and the dollar amount of the loan. The consumer must be made aware that a mortgage is involved, as there must be a description of the security.

We have confined our discussion of needed disclosures to second or junior mortgages; but even though generally exempt, a first mortgage may be covered by these provisions of the Act.

The exclusion relates only to purchase-money first mortgages. That is, those mortgages by which the consumer purchases the home. If there is no mortgage on the home when the owner contracts for a loan or home improvement, the transaction is still covered even though the resulting mortgage is a first lien on the property.

Rescission

Rescission provisions of the Truth-in-Lending law apply generally to real estate transactions. When a consumer uses his place of residence for security for a loan or credit purchase, either directly or indirectly, the transaction is rescindable. There are, however, certain transactions which cannot be cancelled by the debtor. He has no right to cancel a purchase-money first mortgage on the home in which he lives or expects to live. First mortgage transactions involving the financing of the initial construction of the consumer's home or a loan committed before completion of construction of the home to satisfy that construction loan and provide permanent financing cannot be cancelled. These exemptions apply whether or not the consumer previously owned the land on which the home is to be built.

An increase of an outstanding agricultural obligation made under an open-end real estate mortgage or similar lien cannot be cancelled if the debtor was notified of his right to rescind at the time the creditor acquired the mortgage or if such notice was given at any time before the first advance made after June 30, 1969. A lien which becomes subordinated after its creation cannot be cancelled if the debtor didn't have the right to cancel the transaction when it was created.

Generally speaking, then, all second mortgage transactions are covered, while the purchase and ititial financing of a consumer's home are subject to the above explained exemptions.

D.

INSTALLMENT SALES

An installment sale is classified as an "other-than-open-end" transaction. Disclosures required in such transactions must be made before the transaction is consummated, and the creditor must furnish the customer with a duplicate of the instrument or a separate statement by which the required disclosures are made. The disclosure statement must identify the creditor, and all of the disclosures must be made together either on the note or other instrument evidencing the obligation or on a separate instrument which clearly identifies the transaction. If there is more than one signer, obligor, the creditor need not furnish a copy to each. Disclosure to one or the other is sufficient. If, however, there is more than one creditor involved in the transaction, each must clearly be identified and make those disclosures within his knowledge.

As in all disclosure situations, the creditor must retain a copy of the disclosure statement signed by the debtor. The acknowledgment of the copy of the instrument is important as it gives rise to a rebuttal presumption that such was received by the debtor. This presumption becomes important in the trial of an alleged violation of the Act. Even more important, written acknowledgment as proof of receipt of the disclosure statement is conclusive proof of delivery of that instrument as between the original debtor and an assignee of the original creditor. If the assignee of the obligation is without knowledge that the instrument was not in fact delivered, the written acknowledgment of receipt by the debtor constitutes a complete defense to any action brought by the debtor. This does not, however, apply as between the original creditor and the original debtor. Written acknowledgment of the receipt of the instrument as between those parties is, as previously stated, only a rebuttable presumption of delivery.

The general disclosures to be given in an other than open end transaction have already been set forth. However, when a credit sale is involved, the following items must be disclosed along with the other general items of disclosure.

1. The cash price of the property or service purchased. The term "cash price" must be used.
2. The amount of the downpayment, using the term "cash downpayment" or downpayment in property. Any trade-in must be shown and a total sum for cash downpayment along with trade-in must be shown and des-

ignated as "total downpayment."

3. An amount representing the difference between the cash price and the downpayment must be shown and designated as "unpaid balance of cash price."

4. All other charges to be included in the amount financed must be shown and itemized.

5. There must be a sum designated as "unpaid balance," which would be the totals of the unpaid balance of cash price and the other charges.

6. If there are any prepaid finance charges and/or required deposit balances, they must be shown and designated as such.

7. The amount financed designated as such must be shown.

8. Except in the case of a sale of a dwelling, the total amount of the finance charge, with the description of each amount included therein, must be shown. The term "finance charge" must appear. The deferred payment price, designated as such, must likewise appear except in the case of a sale of a dwelling.

In connection with installment sales and other credit sales, the insurance aspects of the Truth-in-Lending Act, both as to credit life insurance and property damage insurance, are important. These have been previously discussed but should be remembered especially in connection with the purchase of durable goods, such as automobiles and household appliances.

E.

MISCELLANEOUS FEATURES

Oftentimes, credit purchases are initiated by mail, telephone, or written communication. In such instances, disclosures must still be made, but the creditor is given additional time to make such disclosures. They must be made not later than the date on which the first payment is due. If the sale initiates from a creditor's catalog or other credit material, the cash price, downpayment, finance charge, deferred payment price, annual percentage rate, and the number, frequency and amount of payments must be set forth or determinable from that catalog. This, of course, ties in with the credit advertising provisions of the Act.

When a loan or other extension of credit is initiated by reason of printed material, the amount of the loan, the finance charge, the total schedule payments, the number, frequency, and amount of payments, and the annual percentage rate for representative amounts or ranges of credit must be set forth in the creditor's printed material distributed to the public. These disclosures can be made in a contract of loan or in such other printed material that is delivered or made available to the customer.

Many times a credit sale is one of a series of transactions made in accordance with an agreement between the debtor and the creditor. If such is the case, disclosures must be made no later than the date the first payment for the particular sale is due. The customer must approve in writing both the annual percentage rate and the method of treating any unearned finance charge on an outstanding balance. The creditor may not retain a security interest in any property on which he has received payments totalling the sales price, including the finance charge, attributable to that specific item of property. When there are a series of payments made on a series of purchases, the first purchase is deemed paid for first; and if there are two or more sales on the same date, the lowest priced item is deemed paid for first.

If a debtor and creditor have entered into a written agreement calling for a series of loans or advances under a single loan, the debtor must approve in writing the annual percentage rate, the method of computing the finance charge, and any other terms of the agreement. The agreement is considered a single transaction, and the disclosures need only be made at the time the agreement is executed.

Other situations which may arise and are particularly treated by the Act include the refinancing, consolidating, or increasing of any extension of credit, an assumption of any obligation, the deferral or extension of an obligation, and the discount for prompt payment. These situations are all treated separately under the Act as to the appropriate time for making disclosures and the disclosures that must be given.

Suffice it to say at this point that the Act itself or Regulation Z should be consulted to the particular obligations of the creditor under each of these circumstances.

Truth-in-Lending violations may be prosecuted civily for a period of two years after the disclosure should have been correctly made. Creditors must keep records for that period. Upon request of the appropriate Federal agency, the creditor must allow inspection of all relevant records and evidence of compliance.

As previously discussed, states which adopt their own disclosure provisions may be exempt from Federal Truth-in-Lending. To date, Maine, Oklahoma and Massachusetts have been granted exemptions in whole or in part.

Chapter IV

FAIR CREDIT REPORTING ACT

Background

Prospective creditors have for many years extensively relied upon credit information accumulation agencies in making a determination of whether credit should be extended to a prospective borrower or credit purchaser. Credit reports are, of course, a prime measure of one's personal integrity and financial dependability. If properly made and maintained as to accuracy, these reports can be a measure of whether or not one can handle his financial obligations conscientiously.

Traditionally, these reports are classified as top secret documents. Only those persons charged with the responsibility of maintaining the information or those persons having access for a legitimate business purpose were entitled to such information. In the normal course of business, credit agencies sell membership to creditors who have regular need for such information and only members have the right to request and receive credit reports.

Unfortunately, there has never been effective legislation to insure the prospective debtor or credit buyer's report was up to date and accurate. It was not an unusual occurrence for one seeking credit to learn his application had been denied on the basis of some information contained in his credit report. Further, the prospective debtor or credit borrower could not obtain the information in his own report and had no redress against the credit agency for the correction of mistakes or the updating of information. The debtor was at the complete mercy of the credit agency and had to rely upon their integrity and their sources of information used in accumulating reports.

One situation within the particular knowledge of this writer occurred several years ago. A person who made his living in real estate, buying and selling, applied for credit at one of the financial institutions. His credit was turned down on the basis of the credit report. Since he was also a member of the credit agency, he was able to obtain the information in the report. The report mistakenly revealed that he had been convicted of statutory rape, and the financial institution passing on his credit felt that such person would be a "poor credit risk." Hence the credit was turned down. Fortunately, the mistake was corrected and credit was extended, but the majority of such cases would find the borrower or credit buyer without redress or even knowledge of why he was rejected.

Subchapter III of the Truth-in-Lending Act, commonly referred to as the Fair Credit Reporting Act, was enacted to remedy many of the inequities of credit reporting. The Truth-in-Lending Act, adopted in October 1970 provided for a 180-day hiatus period before the particular provisions of Subchapter III became effective. Hence, in April 1971 the provisions of the Fair Credit Reporting Act became law.

As is necessary in all Federal legislation, the Congress must justify enactment in terms of constitutional jurisdiction, i.e. such legislation must be within the province of the Federal government under powers designated in the Constitution.

The Fair Credit Reporting Act is based upon constitutional provisions giving the Federal government sole and exclusive jurisdiction over the banking system. In substance, the justification for the Act is that the banking system would be and has been impaired by unfair credit reporting methods. Congress felt that the Fair Credit Reproting Act was necessary to remedy and further prevent such impairments. Further, the legislative background reveals that this legislation was necessary to protect the reputations of consumers. Unless such general reputations were protected and unfair credit reporting methods done away with, there would be a substantial undermining of the public confidence in the banking system.

Congress clearly recognized the elaborate mechanism which has been developed for investigating and evaluating the credit standing of the general consumer. Consumer reporting agencies have assumed a vital role in assembling and evaluating such information. Obviously, a need has arisen to insure that consumer reporting agencies live up to the responsibilities they have undertaken and on the other hand, do nothing to interfere with the consumer's right to privacy. These two objectives may in some instances be incompatible, but each must be accomplished without substantial damage to the other.

The specific purpose of this Act, then, is to regulate and oversee the consumer reporting agencies in their methods of gathering and disclosing credit information.

Prior Judicial Intervention

The judiciary, as well as the legislature, has recognized the inherent problems in credit reporting situations. In the case of Fleck Bros. Co. vs. Sullivan et al., 423 F. 2d. 155 (1970), the court awarded $15,000.00 in compensatory damages and $35,000.00 in punitive damages against a credit agency for publishing libelous statements about a particular consumer. The Fair Credit Reporting Act specifically allows for the granting of compensatory damages, punitive damages and attorneys fees as penalties for those who violate the Act and if effect, follows the courts' rulings made before enactment of the legislation.

Definitions

Like any other piece of legislation, the definitions contained in its sections and the rules of construction applicable to the sections are extremely important for a full understanding of the intent and purpose of the legislation. The following definitions are set forth in Section 1681, 15 U.S.C.A.

"As used in the Act, a person means any individual, partnership, corporation, trust, estate, co-operative, association, government or government-owned subdivision or agency or other entity." That term, then, is all inclusive.

The term consumer, as used in the Act, means any individual.

The term consumer report appears in the Act many times and means any communication of any type (written or oral) given by a consumer reporting agency. These reports pertain to credit worthiness, credit standing, credit capacity, character, general reputation, personal characteristics or mode of living. The information is to be used or expected to be used or collected in whole or in part for the purpose of serving as a factor in establishing the consumer's eligibility for credit or insurance, employment purposes or other permitted uses under the Act.

The Act specifically excludes from its meaning of "consumer report" any corresponsence or communication pertaining solely to transactions between a consumer and the person making the report. Likewise, approval of a specific extension of credit by the issuer of a credit card is excluded from the definition. A third exclusion arises when a party has been requested by a third party to make an extension of credit directly or indirectly to a consumer. If the third party advises the consumer of the name and address of the person to whom the request was made, and such person makes the necessary disclosures, the report will not be included in the term "consumer report."

The Act differentiates the term "consumer report" from "investigative consumer report." The latter means a report on the consumer's character or general reputation obtained through personal interviews with neighbors, friends or associates of the consumer.

Perhaps the most important definition in the statute is that of a consumer reporting agency. That definition set forth verbatim is as follows.

> . . . any person which for monetary fees, dues, or on a cooperative nonprofit basis, regularly engages in whole or in part in the practice of assembling or evaluating consumer credit information or other information on consumers for the purpose of furnishing consumer reports to third parties, and which uses any means of facility of interstate commerce for the purpose of preparing or furnishing consumer reports.

By the definition, the term "consumer reporting agency," is extremely wide in its scope of coverage. It is purposely meant to cover all agencies, small or large, which for a fee or even on a non-profit basis engage in the practice of compiling and disbursing information on consumers, the specific purpose of which agencies is to evaluate or at least assist in the evaluation of a consumer's credit worthiness. Whether or not credit will be extended in a particular case depends upon their accurate recordkeeping and credit evaluation.

Because credit information is often sought by prospective employers, the Act specifically defines and includes "employment purposes." It is a consumer report used for the purpose of evaluating a consumer for either employment, promotion, reassignment, or retention as an employee.

Beyond employment information, many consumer reports contain medical information. Medical information, in the terms of the Act, is that information obtained with the consent of the individual from physicians, hospitals, clinics or the like. Definitions basically provide the scope of the Act. With these in mind, the particular requirements of the Act may be examined.

Reporting Provisions

The Act specifically regulates the purposes for which a consumer reporting agency may provide a consumer report. An agency may provide a report at the insistence of a court having proper jurisdiction to make such order. An agency may furnish such a report upon written request of a consumer. A consumer reporting agency may publish a consumer report to any person who the agency has reason to believe intends to use the information for a proper purpose. When the term "person" is used in the Act, it includes individuals, partnerships, corporations, governmental agencies and other legal entities. Proper purposes for consumer reports include the use of the basis for the extension of credit, renewal of credit, the collection of an outstanding account, employment purposes, the issuance of insurance policies or any other legitimate business purpose. Each of these must, of course, concern the particular consumer about whom inquiry is made. The issuance of a license or other benefit to be extended by a government instrumentality is a further permissable use.

The content of the consumer report is limited by law. Occurrences of bankruptcy more than 14 years previous may not be reported. Suits and judgments more than 7 years old or causes which have expired by operation of the statute of limitations pertaining thereto may not be reported. Accounts of the consumer turned over for collection of more than 7 years old may not be reported. The 7-year limitation also applies to records of arrest, indictment, parole or the like. Also, any item which would be adverse to the consumer and which is more than seven years old must be deleted from the report. There are, however, exceptions to these rules. All the information above listed in terms of age may be reported when the credit transaction can reasonably be expected to involve an amount of $50,000 or more. Where the inquiry stems from an application for insurance which will have a face amount of $50,000 or more, that information may be reported. Where the purpose of the inquiry is employment and such employment can reasonably be expected to generate more than $20,000 per year as an annual salary, the age of the information will not disqualify it from the report.

Disclosures

Like the main provisions of the Consumer Credit Protection Act, the Credit Reporting Act contains disclosure provisions. Any person intending to use or procure a credit report on a prospective borrower or credit buyer, must make certain disclosures to the consumer. The consumer must be made aware that the credit report is being requested. Disclosure of that information must be made in writing and mailed or otherwise delivered to the consumer not later than three days after the date on which the report was requested. The consumer must be aware of the fact that he is entitled to request additional information including the complete nature and scope of the investigation required. The consumer must made a demand for such information within a reasonable time after it has been disclosed to him that the consumer report has been requested. The consumer is entitled to such information not later than five days after he makes such request or not later than five days from the time the report was requested, whichever is the later. The consumer must also be made aware of the fact that a credit report is being sought for employment purposes if he has not specifically applied for that employment opportunity.

The Act, interestingly enough, provides penalties for violation of the disclosure procedures but provides a credit reporting agency with a defense to such action. If the agency can show by a preponderance of the evidence, the greater weight of the evidence, that at the time the alleged violation of the Act took place it had maintained reasonable procedures to assure compliance with those disclosure provisions of the Act, there is no liability.

The Act itself compels the reporting agency to maintain such reasonable procedures. Specifically the agency must obtain the identity of the person seeking the report, the specific purpose for the report, and obtain a certification from that person that the information given will be used for no other than the stated purpose. The agency is held responsible for use of reasonable care in determining that the report will be used for only those purposes allowed by the Act. Consumer reporting agencies are bound by good business practices and by specific provision of the Act to use reasonable procedures to maintain these compilations of information with the greatest degree of accuracy.

The Act also provides that the credit reporting agency must make certain disclosures to governmental agencies upon request. However, the only information they need report is the name of the consumer, his address, his former address, his place of employment, and his former places of employment.

At the time of a request by a consumer, the agency must also disclose its sources of information for preparing any investigative report in the file. The consumer is entitled to clarification from any person to whom reports for employment purposes were given within a two-year period and to whom they were given for any other purpose within a six-month period immediately preceeding the consumer's request for disclosure. The agency is bound to make such disclosures during normal business hours and upon reasonable notice of request from the consumer. The consumer is entitled to this disclosure in person upon furnishing proper identification, or he can obtain the information by telephone if he has previously made a written request for a telephone disclosure. He must further agree to actually pay any charges for such phone communication. When viewing his report, the consumer is entitled to have one other person of his choice with him. The consumer reporting agency is bound to provide some knowledgeable employee for the purpose of explaining the information contained in the report.

Limited Liability

An extremely important provision of the Act is the limitation of civil liability to the consumer reporting agencies for certain types of actions brought by the consumer. These actions, which are limited, include defamation, invasion of privacy, or negligence arising from any information contained in the report. The limitation is an absolute one in that it prohibits the bringing of such suits. This protection from suit inures not only to consumer reporting agencies but also to any user of the information or any person who has furnished information to the agency. However, if the consumer is able to establish that such false information was furnished with malice or willful intent to injure him, he is not limited in his judicial pursuits.

Correction of Errors

Importantly, the consumer upon reading or having disclosed to him the information in his particular report, may dispute the accuracy of any item contained therein. The agency, upon being notified of any alleged error, is then bound to reinvestigate the information. If the facts are found to be inaccurate or no longer can be verified, the agency must delete the information. When an investigation or reinvestigation does not lead to a conclusive finding regarding the disputed fact, the consumer himself may file a brief statement. That statement should set forth the nature of the dispute and, in not more than one hundred words, report the consumer's side of the story. The one hundred word limitation only applies if the agency itself provides a consumer with assistance in writing a summary of that dispute.

Upon receipt of such a written report, the agency is bound to clearly note that the particular item is being disputed. So long as the dispute is not one that is frivolous or irrelevant, it must be clearly identified as a disputed item to any person requesting a report.

The consumer who is successful in showing that an item is no longer accurate or, in fact, can no longer be verified, is entitled to further relief. He may request the agency to notify any person whom the consumer specifically designates as having received a consumer report for employment or other purposes. Persons who have received reports for employment purposes during the past two years may be designated as may any other person who obtained a report for whatever purpose, during the preceding six months. The notification must disclose the fact that the disputed item has been deleted from the file or that the consumer's side of the dispute has been added to the file.

The reporting agency is bound to clearly and conspicuously disclose to the consumer his right to make such a request. Disclosure of such right must be made at the time or prior to the time the information is deleted from the file, or the consumer's statement as above provided is put into the file.

Disclosures made by the consumer reporting agencies must be made without charge to the consumer. However, the consumer must, within thirty days after receipt of notice that a report is being disputed, have made a request for such information as he is entitled to receive. If the consumer does not within that thirty-day period request the information, the consumer reporting agency may impose a reasonable charge for making such disclosures. The agency is, however, bound to advise the consumer as to what the charge will be. In no case may the agency charge more to the consumer than the agency would charge to a person seeking a consumer report in the ordinary course of business. There may not, however, be any charge for notification to persons designated when information is deleted or a disputed statement by the consumer is made part of the file.

Employment Reports

Certain responsibilities are imposed upon consumer reporting agencies when they make reports for employment purposes. Specifically, when matters of public record, such as records of indictments, arrests, convictions, suits, tax liens and outstanding judgments are reported to prospective employers, the agency must notify the consumer that such information is being reported. The consumer must also be made aware of the name and address of the person to whom such information is being reported.

As an alternative to making such disclosure, the agency may maintain strict procedures to insure that the public information being reported for employment purposes is complete and up to date.

Investigative Reports

If the reporting agency is preparing an investigative consumer report, one based on personal interview of friends and associates of the consumer, certain restrictions apply. Information which is a matter of public record can be included in a subsequent consumer report, but information adverse to the consumer may not be included unless verified or received within three months immediately preceding the date upon which the subsequent report is furnished. That is, information accumulated as part of an investigative report must be accurate and verified as being accurate before it can be used in a consumer report.

Adverse Action

A consumer credit report given by a reporting agency may be adverse to the consumer. That report may cause a prospective borrower or credit buyer to be denied such credit. The consumer may be requested to pay a higher rate of interest or he may be denied insurance for personal, family or household purposes. An adverse report may result in a denial of employment. When any of these results are attributable to the adverse report, the person who requested such report must disclose to the consumer the name and address of the reporting agency which made the report. The consumer may avail himself of the rights of disclosure and the right to insure the accuracy of such reports as we have previously discussed.

Adverse results may come from a report prepared by a person other than a consumer reporting agency. When the information contained therein causes the nonextension of credit, the refusal of incurance, or a higher rate of interest, the person requesting such information and acting adversely to the consumer thereon has certain obligations. He must, within a reasonable time after receiving a written request by the consumer, disclose the nature of the information to the consumer who was adversely affected. Written request by the consumer must be made within sixty days after the adverse action is taken. The consumer must also be notified of his right to make such a written request at the time he is advised of the adverse decision.

Again, any person who violates these requirements as to disclosure can extricate himself from liability by showing preponderance of the evidence, that he maintained reasonable procedures to assure the disclosure requirements of this particular phase of the Act would be complied with.

Civil Liability

As mentioned previously, the act contains penalties for those who violate any of its provisions. When a reporting agency, or other person who uses the information, willfully fails to comply with the requirements of the act, he is liable for actual damages (compensatory damages) sustained by the consumer. Punitive damages, as a punishment of the offender, may be awarded by the court.

Since litigation is expensive and necessarily involves attorney fees, the legislature has seen fit to include a provision granting reasonable attorney fees and other costs of the action to the consumer. To obtain this additional relief, the consumer must be successful in the action brought to enforce liability against the reporting agency or other user of the credit information. These provisions were inserted to encourage, rather than to discourage a consumer from exercising his rights under this act.

Subject to the previously explained limitations of liability, a consumer reporting agency or other user of information, may be held liable for negligence and/or for failing to comply with requirements of the act. The act vests the District Courts of the United States with jurisdiction to hear matters arising out of this act irrespective of the amount of money in controversy. Normally, the amount of money in controversy must be ten thousand dollars or more before a United States District Court would have jurisdiction. This, then, is a special situation for the District Courts.

The act also establishes a two year statute of limitations for the bringing of such actions. The statute of limitations begins to run from the time the violation of the act occurs. However, where a credit reporting agency, or other user of the information, has willfully misrepresented any information, the statute of limitations does not begin to run until the consumer discovers that the misrepresentation has been made.

Although the United States District Courts are granted jurisdiction of these matters brought within the allowable period, the action may be brought in any court subject to the local rules of jurisdiction and venue.

Criminal Penalties

In addition to imposing civil liability for violations of the act, the statute also provides criminal penalties. A fine of not more than five thousand dollars or imprisonment for not more than one year, or both, may be imposed upon a person who knowingly or willfully obtains information from a consumer reporting agency under false pretenses. Likewise, the same fine and imprisonment may be imposed upon any officer or employee of a consumer reporting agency who willfully provides information to a person not authorized to receive that information.

Enforcement Agencies

Generally, the Federal Trade Commission has been vested with the authority and responsibility of enforcing compliance with these particular provisions of the Consumer Credit Protection Act. The Federal Reserve Board, the Federal Deposit Insurance Corporation, Federal Savings and Loan Insurance Corporation, Federal Administrator of the National Credit Union Administration, The Civil Aeuronautics Board, and the Secretary of agriculture are also vested with responsibilities of compliance in those particular situations which affect their areas of responsibility.

Like other provisions of the Consumer Credit Protection Act, state laws concerning fair credit reporting may take precedent over the federal legislation, if the state seeks and obtains an exemption. The state law must, of course be substantially the same as the federal act or more restrictive.

Conclusion

These, then, are the substantive provisions of the Fair Credit Reproting Act. They are bound to have wide, sweeping effects not only upon credit reporting agencies, but also upon other financial institutions and associations of dealers who necessarily rely upon credit reporting agencies and credit reports in the selling of their goods.

One negative effect has already been felt. Banks participate in V.A. and F.H.A. guaranteed loan programs. Under such programs, these institutions could be classified as credit reporting agencies and subject to the civil and criminal penalties provided in the act. Necessarily, V.A. and F.H.A. loans require banks to charge lower than normal mortgage rates and involve expensive paper work in preparing the loans. Many of the banks have expressed concern with the added possibility of civil and criminal exposure for violation of the act. Consequently, many banks have indicated that V.A. and F.H.A. loans are no longer desirable ventures. Senator William Proxmire, sponsor of the Fair Credit Reporting Act has expressed his opinion that the banks are simply making an excuse to rid themselves of the F.H.A. and V.A. programs. It has been suggested that the act be amended to exempt banks from the credit reporting agency classification. This would deprive the banks of their excuse for turning down such transactions. The answer to this particular problem is not yet clear.

It should be restated that the Fair Credit Reporting Act, like the other provisions of the Consumer Credit Protection Act, is aimed at the consumer transaction. It is meant to protect the consumer and to enhance his chances of obtaining credit for personal and family needs, if his past history of credit worthiness is such as to make him a good credit risk. Accurate and fair credit reporting will not only protect the individual consumer, but also the creditor who can more intelligently make credit decisions.

Chapter V

WHERE THE CONSUMER
MAY NOT BE PROTECTED

A.

UNIFORM COMMERCIAL CODE

The Uniform Commercial Code was developed by the Conference and Institute of Commissioners on the Uniform State Laws. It was adopted and endorsed by the American Bar Association in the fall of 1951 and enacted into the law of Pennsylvania in 1953. Since that time, there have been many modifications to the Code and it has been adopted in most states. The Uniform Commercial Code is important in its applications to consumer transactions involving sale of goods both as to secured and unsecured transactions.

The Uniform Commercial Code provides buyers and sellers certain remedies for breach of contract. Covered are such areas as breach of warranty (both expressed and implied), breach of a secured creditor's rights in collateral property, and rights of consumer debtors against financial institutions who, in the normal course of business, buy negotiable instruments from creditors or credit sellers.

Although the Uniform Commercial Code was adopted in many respects for the specific purpose of regulating sales between businessmen and for regulating the flow of commercial paper and securities, the scope of our examination of the Uniform Commercial Code will be limited to those sections dealing with the consumer and his credit transactions.

Negotiable Notes

In the normal consumer credit transaction and especially

one which is an installment purchase, the debtor is obligated and instructed to sign a cognovit or promissory note. Since most sellers of merchandise are not in a position to finance their own transactions, they discount or assign the notes signed by debtors to banks or other financial institutions in return for instant cash.

Basically, a cognovit note is a negotiable instrument if it is an instrument signed by the maker thereof containing an unconditional order or promise to pay a sum certain in money, payable on demand or at a definite time to the person named thereon or to the bearer of the instrument.

Payment of the note may not be conditional upon the happening of an event. If it is conditional, the note will not be negotiable. We will discover the importance of an instrument being negotiable, as its negotiable character may effect the relationship between the debtor and the financial institution which, in good faith and without any knowledge of defect in the product or the like, purchases that note from the original seller of the goods or services.

The fact that the note contains stated interest or states that it is to be paid in installments does not make it a non-negotiable instrument. Further, the note may provide, if allowable in the particular jurisdiction where it is executed, that costs of collections, attorneys fees and court costs may be collected upon default. As previously stated, the instrument must be payable in a definite time and may be subject to acceleration if a payment is in default.

The note must be payable to its bearer to the order of an ascertainable person or his assignee. A negotiable instrument, such as a promissory note, may be assigned just as a check may be endorsed. Normally, when there is an assignment made in the course of the credit transaction, the original creditor warrants to the assignee that the note is collectible and will be paid on time. Notes are usually sold to the banks or other financial institutions with recourse. That is, the bank may look to the original creditor for payment if the borrower does not pay according to the terms of the contract or note.

Holder in Due Course

If a bank or other financial institution takes the instrument for value, in good faith and without notice that it is already overdue or has been dishonored or that there has been any defense or claim on the part of the debtor against the original creditor, that financial institution becomes a holder in due course. It does not become a holder in due course if it takes the note by purchase at a judicial sale, by legal process, by acquiring it in the taking over of an estate, or by purchasing it as part of a bulk transaction not in the regular course of business of the transferor.

Without examining each and every one of the elements of a holder in due course, it is sufficient to say that each element is the subject of a specific section of the Uniform Commercial Code. Each is subject to considerable judicial interpretation. The existence of each depends upon the particular facts and circumstances surrounding the transaction.

The significance of being a holder in due course is substantially that a holder in due course takes the instrument, the promissory note, free from all claims on the part of any person, and free from all defenses to the note of any party of the instrument with whom the holder has not dealt. As against a holder in due course, the debtor may raise defenses pertaining only to his incapacity to enter into the original contract, duress or illegality of a transaction. Each of these, if successfully pursued, renders the entire transaction null and void.

The holder in due course is still bound to recognize any discharge in insolvency or bankruptcy proceedings which the debtor may have obtained. Likewise, he is bound by any other discharge of which he had notice when he took the instrument.

Conversely to the rights of a holder in due course, one who is merely a holder of the instrument is bound by any valid claim that the original debtor may have had. Similarly he is subject to all defenses which the debtor had against the original creditor. For instance, if John Smith were to buy a refrigerator from the ABC Furniture store and the store sold that note to the Ace Finance Company, the Ace Finance Co., if fulfilling all the elements of the holder in due course, would take that instrument free of any defense John Smith would have had against the furniture company. If the product were defective or if the furniture company failed to live up to its warranties, John Smith would have no recourse against the finance company. No matter if the refrigerator broke down that first day that John Smith had it, he would be subject to a lawsuit brought by the finance company and would have to pay the balance due and owing on the note. He would, of course, have recourse against the original seller of the product; but in many cases, that seller is no longer in business or the claim is uncollectible.

The Federal Trade Commission has recently conducted hearings throughout the United States regarding complaints from consumers. It has been found that the situation above described is not an exception but is rather commonplace. Among the complaints was one story of a woman who purchased a washing machine for $361.00. In a few months, the machine started to leak. After eleven calls to the appliance store yielded no results, she still remained obligated to pay the finance company, which bought her note, for a total of $475.00. That figure included the cost of the machine, interest and other loan-associated charges.

There is now considerable pressure being applied to state legislatures and Congress to enact legislation which would do away with the holder in due course concept. President Nixon's consumer affairs advisor has told the Federal Trade Commission to do whatever is necessary to protect the consumer from this situation. Since the holder in due course concept has been adopted in most states, it will require a great deal of legislation to reverse the status quo. Of course, there will be considerable pressure applied by banks, finance companies and the like to retain the holder in due course principles. Absent this safeguard, these institutions will find themselves in a constant state of litigation. It appears that both the consumer and the financial institutions must be more selective in their choice of business bedfellows.

The procedure by which a holder in due course, or for that matter, the original payee, takes judgment on the note is relatively simple. The only burden that the plaintiff has is to present the note to the court with written claim that a certain amount is due thereunder. A signature on a note is presumed to be genuine or authorized. Unless the signature is denied, all that a holder in due course need do is to produce the instrument. If there is a defense on the part of the maker of the note, he has the burden of establishing that defense. Once the defense is presented, the holder in due course has the burden of rebutting it. Since defenses against holders in due course are limited basically to fraud and incapacity of the party to make the note, the chances are that the creditor will prevail in the great majority of cases.

B.

COGNOVIT NOTES

Incident to most credit transactions is the signing of a cognovit note by the buyer. Basically, a cognovit note is one which contains a confession of judgment clause. That is, the credit buyer agrees that upon the happening of a condition (his default in payment), he authorizes any attorney at law, acting ostensibly on his behalf but at the insistence of the creditor or other holder of the instrument, to confess a judgment against him. By signing such a note, the credit buyer or borrower gives up his right of appeal and authorizes any attorney at law to sign a confession of judgment against him. Of course once the judgment is issued, then the creditor may take those steps necessary to effectuate its collection. These steps include garnishment of wages, a lien upon any real estate owned by the debtor, attachment of property and other judicial process resulting in the sale or sequestering of the debtor's property.

The Truth-in-Lending Act has limited the operation and effect of the cognovit note in terms of the resulting judgment lien on the principal place of residence of the debtor. However, some states have taken furhter action at least to make the debtor aware of the nature of the instrument he is signing. These states insist that certain warnings appear on the face of the note.

Ohio, for example, provides that the following writing must be clearly and conspicuously placed on the document:

> WARNING! By signing this paper you give up your
> right to notice and court trial. If you do not pay
> on time, a court judgment may be taken against
> you without your prior knowledge and the powers
> of the court can be used to collect from you or your
> employer regardless of any claims you may have
> against the creditor whether for returned goods,
> faulty goods, failure on his part to comply with
> agreement, or any other cause.

This notice, then, at least puts the debtor on notice as to

what he is giving up by signing the note. If the warning does not appear, the creditor may not use the note to obtain a judgment. The failure of the note does not, however, affect the validity of the underlying obligation.

The same statute provides the procedure under which a cognovit judgment may be taken. A petition of complaint is filed on behalf of the creditor in which the attorney who represents the creditor must include a statement setting forth that to the best of his knowledge, the last known address of the defendant is shown in the complaint. The reason for this is that immediately after the court has rendered a judgment, the defendant debtor is entitled to notice that the judgment has been taken against him. This particular statute of Ohio provides that the court must notify the defendant by personal service or by registered or certified mail at his last known address as set forth in the petition. This notice allows the debtor to take whatever timely action necessary and proper to have the judgment set aside or vacated.

Most states provide that if a judgment is taken upon a cognovit note without notice to the debtor and in fact the judgment taken was for an amount more than actually due, then the judgment may be set aside. If the judgment is set aside, the debtor is entitled to file an answer in the matter setting forth any defense that he may have. Of course, as discussed more fully, if the judgment creditor is a holder in due course of the negotiable cognovit note, defenses that the debtor had as against the seller of the goods may not be enforceable as against the holder in due course.

The judgment creditor is, of course, bound by procedural requirements and requirements of jurisdiction and venue. For example, Ohio requires that the judgment be taken against the maker of the note or any one of the several makers of the note in the territorial jurisdiction of a municipal court where one or more of the makers resides or where the warrant of attorney, the cognovit provision, was executed. This procedural requirement affords the debtor a better chance of actually learning about the judgment within a reasonable time after it is taken. Defenses of lack of jurisdiction are available to the judgment debtor against the judgment creditor no matter if the creditor is a holder in due course or not.

Cognovit notes are often erroneously referred to as judgment notes. Judgment notes are usually restricted to negotiable instruments, while cognovit notes generally may be negotiable or non-negotiable. Many states simply do not allow the confession of judgments upon cognovit notes or judgment notes and require a full hearing on the underlying obligation. Among these states are Georgia and Alabama.

Other states restrict the use of confession of judgment provisions in various ways. Arkansas provides that the debtor must appear in open court with the assent of the creditor to confess judgment.

In California a judgment can be confessed by a signed verified statement of the debtor.

Colorado does not allow a confession of judgment on a note signed in connection with an installment contract for the purchase of a motor vehicle.

Confessions of judgment are not permitted in Hawaii if the transaction was a time sale.

Obligations arising out of home repair contracts cannot give rise to confessions of judgment in Maine. In New York a judgment may be confessed upon a debtor's affidavit. Confessions are invalid before a debtor's default on installment contracts for $1,500 or less. These installment contracts must be for the purchase of goods by the ultimate consumer as opposed to a business or commercial transaction. Generally, a power of attorney provision for confession of judgment is prohibited in retail installment contracts.

Along with the actual judgment, the cognovit debtor may find himself responsible for court costs and attorney fees. The majority of states do not permit the creditor to recover attorney fees, but a few states do.

It is apparent that confession of judgment provisions differ from jurisdiction to jurisdiction. Every consumer should be aware of the basic aspects of his state's particular statute.

<u>C</u>.

WARRANTIES AND CONSUMER SELF-HELP

We are dealing primarily with consumer credit transactions and many of these, if not the majority, have to do with

54

the sale of goods. It is, therefore, important to consider warranties.

Express warranties are those made by any affirmation of fact or promise which relates to the goods or any description of the goods which has been made part of the basis of the bargain. Express warranties can be made by the showing of any sample or model of the goods, upon which the buyer relies in purchasing that particular item. Express warranties can be made either orally or written, and the courts have gone so far as to say that mass media advertising as to the quality of an item constitutes an express warranty.

Express warranties take precedence when inconsistent with a seller's attempt to disclaim them. Any attempt to disclaim an express warranty will fail unless the disclaimer refers specifically to the representation made. Contracts which state that all express warranties are disclaimed are usually held to be against public policy as to that provision and the express warranty will stand.

There are basically two types of implied warranties: that the goods are fit for the particular purpose for which they are intended, and that the goods are merchantable. An attempted disclaimer of the implied warranty of merchantability must conspicuously state that such warranty is disclaimed before it will be effective. Likewise, a disclaimer of the warranty of fitness must be in writing and conspicuous. The reason for conspicuous writing is that there is a disparity of bargaining position between a consumer and a credit seller. Consumers more often than not don't read the contracts they sign and can't reasonably be expected to. A creditor must, therefore, take it upon himself to notify the consumer in writing that he is waiving certain of his rights.

Often times a consumer credit purchaser finds that there has been a breach of warranty either expressed or implied as pertains to the goods he has purchased. The holder in due course concept, as explained above, is important in that a breach of warranty cannot be, under the current state of the law, asserted against the holder in due course of the instrument of indebtedness.

The consumer buyer has by state legislation certain remedies with respect to breach of warranties.

These remedies may allow for recovery of money damages

for the defect in the product itself or if the product defect results in injury to a member of the buyer's household or guest, compensation for that personal injury.

The Uniform Commercial Code provides that a buyer may recover for breach of warranty an amount equal to the diminution of value of the goods attributable to the breach of warranty. That is, he may recover the difference in the value of the goods measured by what they would have been worth had they been as warranted and what they were actually worth with the defective condition. This remedy is applicable whether the goods were defective by reason of express or implied warranties.

The courts, then, are vested with jurisdiction and power to redress grievances for breach of warranty. Although it may be somewhat far afield from the concept of regulation of consumer credit, it is important to mention a development in society which has taken place in relation to redressing grievances for breach of warranty.

Organizations have entered into concerted activities in attempts to coerce sellers to honor warranties. In some instances, this type of procedure involving picketing and the distribution of literature to discourage consumers from dealing with a particular retailer or manufacturer may be justified. Often time, this bypassing of our judicial system amounts to civil extortion and should be prohibited.

The industry hardest hit by mass action has been the automotive. Both manufacturers and dealers have felt the wrath. Traditionally, efforts by unhappy consumers to air their grievances have been thwarted by the courts.

In Carter v. Knapp Motors Company, 243 Ala. 600, 11 S. 2d. 383 (1943), the consumer feeling that he had purchased an unsatisfactory automobile, painted a white elephant on it and parked it in front of the dealer's showroom. In that case, the court held that the right to conduct business without the wrongful interference of others is a valuable property right which will be protected by the injunctive process and specifically held the dealer in that case entitled to an injunction;

In Menard v. Houle, 298 Mass. 546, 11 NE 2d. 436 (1937), a consumer was enjoined from parking his car contiguous to the dealer's showroom when such car was painted with signs such as "Don't believe what they say. This car is no good." In that case, the court applied its equity jurisdiction as there was a continuing course of unjustified and wrongful conduct motivated by malice and done with the intent of causing damage to the dealer's business. In such case, there is no adequate remedy at law.

In Saxson Motor Sales v. Torino, 166 Misc. 863, 2 NYS 2d. 885 (1938), the consumer was enjoined from parking his car in front of the dealer's premises with signs on its sides, which signs attacked the quality of the car. The court therein held that the consumer's conduct was no different than an attempt to interfere with the dealer by means of some physical obstruction.

As recently as January, 1971, a New York court applied these principles in granting an automobile dealer's request for a temporary restraining order. Tappan Motors, Inc. v. Waterbury, 318 NYS 2d. 125 (1971).

In the Tappan case, supra., a dissatisfied consumer parked his vehicle in front of the dealer's place of business for about three hours. Signs on the car stated he had purchased the auto from the dealer and that over thirty repairs had not been made. A phone number was provided for those who sought additional information.

The New York Court, in granting the temporary restraining order, held:

> The right to carry on a lawful business without obstruction is a property right and acts committed without just cause or excuse which interfere with the carrying on of the plaintiff's business or destroy its custom, its credit or its profits, do an irreparable injury and thus authorize the issuance of an injunction. P. 126.

Contrary to these holdings, there is currently developing a body of law which gives unlimited license to consumers and organized groups of consumers to voice their grievances and compel the honoring of warranties, whether justifiably or not. The Sypreme Court of the United States has specifically held that the distribution of literature no matter its truth or falsity may not be enjoined. Thus, consumers now apparently have a remedy outside of judicial process for enforcing warranties. The results and benefits of allowing our courts to be bypassed remain to be seen.

Chapter VI

STATE REGULATIONS

Small Loan Acts

In addition to the state usury laws, most states have enacted other legislation to govern particular loan transactions. State laws include Small Loan Acts, Consumer Finance Acts, and Industrial Loan Acts. Each of these seeks to regulate a particular transaction as to, among other things, the amount that can be lent and the interest that can be charged.

Most states regulate the period of time over which the small loan may be extended. A small loan usually extends up to about $5000, but most state acts cover extensions of credit from $600 to $1500. The acts provide for the licensing of lenders and require the payment of fees for such licenses.

Among the other features of the various acts are prescrubed methods for computing interest and finance charges, regulation of rebates for prepayments, arrangement for credit life and other types of insurances in connection with the loan, reporting requirements by the lenders, and penalties for violation of the acts.

It must be remembered that the small loan acts of the various states must not be in conflict with the Consumer Credit Protection Act. The more stringent as far as reporting and disclosure requirements will take precedence. While many small loan acts permit the lender to sell insurance along with the loan, Truth-in-Lending requirements as to inclusion in the amount financed and insurance disclosure statements must accompany the transaction. Insurance provisions under the various acts vary from state to state. Some allow credit life on loans of more than specified amounts. Some allow the sale of such when there is pledged collateral. Many states allow credit life and health, accident and property damage insurance to be sold when there is pledged tangible personal property. The variations are too numerous to set forth, but the consumer should be aware that insurance coverage may be available to him when he obtains a small loan.

Penalties for violation of the act differ from state to state, but many provide that the entire transaction will be null and void if the lender charges in excess of the allowed rate. Often, fines and even imprisonment are the costs to be paid for willful violations. Computation of the allowable rate is, of course, the most complicated aspect of each act. The allowable rates usually include all loan expenses as well as interest and service charges. Many states provide that stated rates may be charged on stated balance of principal. That is, for example, three per cent may be charged on the first three hundred of principal, two per cent on the next two hundred, and one per cent on the balance. Other states prescribe a flat maximum on the loan, and still others outline in great detail allowable service charges, default charges, and other loan-related expenses. Some states allow a discounting of the loan while others frown upon it.

Suffice it to say, that the variations found in these acts are tremendous, but each is important to consumers who seek a loan. Awareness of at least the existence of these acts is mandatory for any intelligent borrower.

Credit Insurance

Mention has already been made of the availability of credit life insurance in connection with a consumer credit or loan transaction. Nearly all states regulate credit life insurance through state legislation. The regulations may be set forth in special statutes or contained as part of the Small Loan Acts. The purpose of credit life insurance is twofold. First, it protects the consumer and his family from having to pay off an obligation after the primary supplier of the family has died. Of- financial ten this task becomes impossible and results in repossession of the collateral, if any, or sale of pledged property. Secondly, credit life insurance is a form of protection to the lender. Once the head of the household is deceased, the chances of collection of the loan are severely decreased. Thus if there is credit life insurance, the creditor will be paid immediately and will avoid costly collection fees, attorney's fees and the like.

In addition to credit life, the debtor may want to insure himself against other risks which would prevent him from repaying the loan or the extended credit. Health, accident or disability insurance may be available in connection with the transaction.

State regulation usually includes maximums on the amount of available coverage, period of time of coverage, premiums, and permissable issuers. Over-all supervision of credit life insurance is usually vested in the superintendent of insurance of each state.

Again, credit life insurance is somewhat regulated by the Federal Consumer Credit Protection Act. Disclosure of its cost must be made, and the cost thereof must be included in the amount financed. Technical violation of these provisions occurs often, as many financial institutions, while claiming to provide this coverage free to its customers, have built the cost thereof into their basic financing rates. These financial institutions usually have purchased a form of group coverage for all their accounts so as to protect themselves as fully as possible.

Check Loans

Credit may be extended by banks by simply allowing customers to write checks on accounts not having sufficient funds. This type of credit may be called "check loans" or "advance loans."

Those states which permit such loans, have by legislation, regulated the procedures. Maximum charges, late payments, service charges, monthly payments and penalties are all closely regulated. Agreements between the banks and their customers give rise to this type of credit. The terms of the agreement likewise are regulated by state statute, especially as to the maximum amount of the loan.

Since this type of agreement is an extension of credit, the transaction is giverned by the Consumer Credit Protection Act. Proper disclosures, before the actual extension of credit, must be given.

Pawnbrokers

Credit may be extended by pawnbrokers. State statutes

regulate the interest rates he may charge as well as prescribing recordkeeping requirements. Further provisions of state statutes dictate the procedures which the pawnbroker must follow if he wishes to sell the property after the debt has matured and the borrower has failed to redeem his property.

Usury

All of the several states of the United States have usury laws. These prohibit the lending of money or the extending of credit at a rate of interest higher than that prescribed by statute. There are several types of interest regulations--those pertaining to contract rates, those pertaining to judgments, and those pertaining to legal rates of interest. Most states prescribe maximum interest rates falling in the range of from four per cent to eight per cent. The state statutes also generally provide a penalty for charging more than the allowable rate of interest. These penalties can take the form of a forfeiture of all of the interest or some multiple of the interest. A few states provide that the contract itself shall be null and void.

The contract rate of interest is that rate of interest which the parties dealing in an arm's length transaction have agreed upon. A judgment rate of interest is that rate of interest that may be collectible by a judgment creditor on a judgment rendered by a court of competent jurisdiction. The legal rate of interest is that rate fixed by law in the particular state. Most states, in applying their usury laws, exempt corporations from the operation thereof, and the corporation is bound to pay that rate of interest it negotiates for in any contract for purchase of goods or services. Corporations are normally, however, bound by the legal or judgment rates of interest provided in the usury statutes.

Ohio, for instance, provides that the legal rate of interest is six per cent; the contract rate of interest that may be agreed upon by the parties, excluding the corporation, is eight per cent; and the rate of interest that may be applied against a judgment debtor is six per cent. Ohio provides no penalty for usurious charges but rather provides in Section 1343.04 that any usurious charges shall be applied as against principal rather than interest. There are certain other exceptions to the usury statutes, such as building and loan associations under the Ohio law, which may charge a rate of interest greater than that provided for by statute.

The purpose of the usury laws is, of course, self-explanatory. Since there was no usury law at common law, absent a state statute, the parties could agree upon any rate of interest they so desired. The adoption of usury laws was an effort by the state legislatures to protect the borrower or the credit buyer from having to pay an exhorbitant price for money. Absent such statutes, those persons who needed money the most would have to pay the highest rate of interest and correspondingly, those people would be the persons least able to afford such payments. Unless there is specific definition in the usury statute as to whom the law applies, it would apply equally to all individuals, financial institutions, finance companies and the like in their practice of loaning money to individuals. National banks which are governed by Federal statute are empowered by such statute to lend money at a rate of interest not exceeding the usury laws of the particular state in which they are located.

Usury laws and their application can become quite complicated. For instance, the computation of interest in the discounting of paper may or may not lead to usurious interest, and the method of computation and how the interest is compounded certainly leads to a different effective rate of interest. It is not the purpose here to discuss all these applications, but merely to make the reader aware of the existence of such laws and to understand their general nature.

Most usury statutes require that a punishable violation of the law must be intentional on the part of the lender. He must have intended to violate the law; and beyond the intention there must be, of course, a greater rate of interest charged than is allowed by the law.

Intention is, of course, a nebulous term and must be found to exist from the circumstances surrounding the transaction. The courts view the entire transaction in determining intention of the creditor. Commissions and other expenses may be listed as charges separate and apart from the interest, but if these are found to be only a means of evading the particular state's usury laws and in fact are additional interest charges, the loan may be found to be usurious.

Generally speaking, a charge of usury cannot arise out of any transaction other than a loan of money or forebearance on a past loan. Thus, sale of property on credit is not subject to the usury laws unless the transaction is a sham to evade the usury laws. A transaction may be usurious even though the borrower is not to repay in money at a rate of interest higher than the usury law permits. If the borrower is also to repay by means of property or services, the value of which exceeds the legal rate of interest, then the transaction would be usurious. Whether or not the contract is usurious may depend upon whether the interest is taken in advance; the length of period over which the principal and interest are payable; whether or not there is an increase in interest after the loan matures; or whether the loan may be accelerated by default; and how interest is compounded. Again, these transactions become quite complicated and the courts throughout the several states are not in agreement as to the effect of these various elements upon the legality of the contract as far as usury is concerned. It would take a detailed study of each state's usury law plus judicial interpretation of that law to set forth any general rules concerning each and every one of these elements.

It is important to note that the determination of whether or not a contract is usurious is made at the date of its consummation. There can be no transaction between the parties at a later date which would cure the contract if it is in fact usurious at its inception. If a contract is found to be usurious, the debtor is, under the particular state statute, granted certain methods of redress. As previously stated, many state statutes provide for the forfeiture of the amount of interest or a penalty in some multiple of the rate of interest. This penalty is to be paid by the creditor to the debtor. In certain circumstances, the debtor may be estopped or may waive his rights to claim benefit under the usury statutes. There may be unusual circumstances in which the debtor has done something to forfeit his rights.

Some states allow the vacation of the contract in equity by the debtor as a penalty for violation of the usury laws. This would be available if the debtor has no adequate remedy at law which would enable him to be compensated in damages for the usurious conduct of the creditor. Most states simply allow the debtor to set off against the principal the amount of usurious interest that he has paid. When a statute provides a remedy, it is the exclusive remedy that the debtor has and may be affected by a statute of limitations. Remedies may be available to assignees of the debtor depending upon the particular jurisdiction where the issue is raised.

Most states do not declare the contract which is usurious to be void. The statutes merely provide a remedy for the buyer or borrower. The National Banking Act, for instance, makes the bank subject to liability in twice the amount of the interest received if such interest was usurious. The question of usury usually arises when a creditor seeks to enforce his judicial rights as against the debtor. At that time, the debtor, if the contract is in fact usurious, must raise it as a defense and it becomes a question of law and fact by the jury to determine whether or not the contract was in fact usurious. Usury may or may not be a criminal offense depending upon the particular jurisdiction where the question is raised.

Primary features of state usury laws are set forth in Table A. which follows.

TABLE A

STATE USURY RATES

STATE	Legal Rate %	Contract Rate %
Alabama	6	8
Alaska	6	9
Arkansas	6	10
California	7	10
Colorado	6	no maximum if in writing, 16% on loans over $2,000.
Connecticut	6	12
Delaware	6	9
Dist. of Col.	6	8
Florida	6	10
Georgia	7	8
Idaho	6	10
Hawaii	6	1% per mo.
Indiana	8	8

64

STATE	Legal Rate %	Contract Rate %
Iowa	5	9
Kansas	6	10
Kentucky	6	7
Louisiana	7	8
Maine	6	no max. if in writing to corp.
Maryland	6	8
Massachusetts	6	no limit if in writing
Michigan	5	7
Minnesota	5	7
Mississippi	6	8
Missouri	6	8
Montana	6	10
Nebraska	6	10
Nevada	7	12
New Hampshire	6	no limit if in writing
New Jersey	7 1/2	7 1/2
New Mexico	6	10
New York	7 1/2	7 1/2
North Carolina	6	8
North Dakota	4	9
Ohio	6	8
Oklahoma	6	10
Oregon	6	10
Pennsylvania	6	6
Rhode Island	6	21
South Carolina	6	8% plus additional interest on loans over $50,000.
South Dakota	6	10
Tennessee	6	10
Texas	6	10
Utah	6	10
Vermont	7 1/2	7 1/2

STATE	Legal Rate %	Contract Rate %
Virginia	6	8
Washington	6	12
West Virginia	6	6
Wisconsin	5	12
Wyoming	7	10

This chart does not reflect all of the possible variables in the contract rate of interest. Many states have enacted legislation which provides a range of allowable interest charges by contract depending upon whether or not the contract is in writing and the amount of the loan. The chart does however reflect the most prevalent charges in consumer type transactions.

Chapter VII

COLLECTION OF DELINQUENT CREDIT ACCOUNTS

Entwined with the regulation of credit which we have already discussed is, of course, the regulation of the creditor's rights to collect accounts which become delinquent and the protections afforded a debtor. The coverage of this subject will be limited, as it is the subject of extensive coverage elsewhere in this series. (See Morganstern, S., Legal Protection in Garnishment and Attachment.)

Basically, the rights of creditors in the collection of delinquent accounts are regulated by state and in some instances federal legislation. A creditor after reducting an obligation to judgment has several options as to the course of procedure he wishes to follow. Collection attempts may take the form of garnishment of wages or garnishment of assets other than wages including bank accounts, life insurance, partnership property, equitable interests, decedent estates, stock and bonds, pensions and the like. The creditor may invoke the process of attachment for judgment both as to wages and other items of personalty and real property if the strict statutory procedure for same is followed.

The Consumer Credit Protection Act regulates the garnishment of wages as to the amount which can be taken from a debtor's wages and the effect that a garnishment may have upon a consumer's employment. Basically, an employee cannot now be discharged from his employment by reason of the fact that his wages have been garnished for any one indebtedness. This is a substantial protection and, of course, was enacted to protect the debtor from losing his job by reason of the fact that he could not meet his financial obligations. Suffice it to say at this point that the regulation of wage garnishments has been severely tightened from what it used to be and as a practical matter, has been severely restricted. The costs involved to the creditor in the way

67

of court costs and attorney fees, in most instances, outweigh the amount that can be taken from an employee's wages.

Although the procedures of attachment and garnishment may be instituted by creditors, debtors are not without protection under the law. Nearly all states provide property exemptions when property is taken pursuant to a levy of execution on a judgment or by attachment. These exemptions may be negligible in some instances, or in other instances, quite comprehensive and cover items of personal property, household goods, wages and other such items as surrender value of life insurance policies.

Effectively, the Consumer Credit Protection Act has provided an exemption for one's principal place of residence. As has been previously explained, certain transactions would, under the Consumer Credit Protection Act be rescindable, if the creditor acquires a security interest directly or indirectly in the consumer's principal place of residence. To avoid this, many potential creditors have specifically waived the right to such a lien in return for having the transaction nonrescindable. Accordingly, if and when a judgment is taken, a judgment lien cannot be placed upon the principal place of residence, and the Consumer Credit Protection Act has, in effect, built in an exemption for such property. In addition thereto, many states provide a homestead exemption. This exemption may be represented as a specified amount of value of the principal place of residence of a judgment debtor.

Prior to the enactment of the Consumer Credit Protection Act, the garnishment of wages was regulated strictly by state statute. Now the amount of exempted wages is to be computed in compliance with the Consumer Credit Protection Act or state laws, whichever are more restrictive. Likewise, state laws may provide for stricter provisions with regard to the discharge of an employee by reason of garnishment of his wages. In any event, the Consumer Credit Protection Act has sought to remedy the situation where a consumer having problems managing his financial life is further endangered by garnishment of wages.

The particular state statutes and procedural requirements must be followed strictly by a creditor when attempting to collect on a defaulted obligation. The Uniform Commercial Code likewise must be consulted when the transaction is a secured one. That is, in certain instances, the creditor may have taken personal property as security for a loan or extension of credit. The creditor must comply with the codified requirements including certain notice provisions when he attempts to use that collateral as payment or partial payment for the obligation. Perhaps the most prevalent instance is the sale of an automobile. As a matter of course, the financial institution extending the credit takes the automobile as security for the loan. In most instances, a lien is placed on the title of the automobile and is notice to the world and all persons dealing with that automobile that the financial institution is financially interested in the automobile and such has been taken as collateral. Most states have adopted auto title laws. Only a lien noted upon the title is sufficient to attach any kind of interest in the automobile.

If and when there has been a default on the obligation secured by the automobile, the bank or other financial institution has the right to immediate possession thereof. This is usually done by repossession, oftentimes stealthily and without notice to the debtor. Once the automobile is in the possession of the bank or financial institution, it may be sold at public or private sale. The Uniform Commercial Code provides that if the creditor wishes to proceed against the debtor for any deficiency which may arise as a result of the sale of the automobile for a price less than is owed on the obligation, the debtor must be given written notice of the sale. Such notice must contain the minimum price at which the auto is to be sold for, and the time and place of sale. In the absence of such notification, any deficiency would be expunged.

These provisions of the Uniform Commercial Code apply not only to automobiles, but to any chattel held as security for an obligation and to be sold at public or private sale. Although the Uniform Commercial Code gives a secured creditor the right to sell at private sale, if he wishes to proceed on a deficiency, the sale must be a public sale with the notices above explained.

Without reviewing in further detail any of the procedures available to a creditor for collection of an account, it is important to note that such procedures are available. These procedures may result in the attachment or garnishment of personal, real or intangible property owned by the debtor.

Statutes of Limitations

A statute of limitation sets a time limitation in which a

69

suit must be instituted. Once that limitation has expired, a defendant may raise the expiration of the statutory time as an absolute defense to any action brought by the creditor in an attempt to collect the debt. Since statutes of limitations do not prohibit a creditor from instituting suit, a debtor must affirmatively raise the issue as a defense. Failure to answer the suit or raise the issue will result in a waiver of that defense.

The Consumer Credit Protection Act provides that all actions for violations must be brought within two years of the violation. This period can, in effect, be shortened if the creditor complies with correction procedures contained in the Act and previously described.

Each state has its own set of statutes of limitations (See Table B). These statutes govern a wide range of types of suits from breach of contract to tort. We are only concerned with those affecting consumer credit, but an awareness of the existence of the comprehensiveness of these statutes is imperative to every consumer.

Basically, the statutes of limitations which affect consumer credit are those governing the bringing of actions under contracts (oral, written or under seal), promissory notes, open accounts and judgments. The period of limitation on each of these types of obligations varies from state to state. Contract periods of limitations range from three years to twenty years depending upon the state, while actions on promissory notes are viable from three to seventeen years, depending upon the particular jurisdiction. Actions on open accounts must usually be brought within a shorter period of time than a written contract of promissory note, and the period ranges between three and eight years.

A judgment which is, of course, the result of a lawsuit may not remain effective forever. Many states provide that if no collection is made on the judgment within a stated time, it will expire. Such periods vary from five to twenty years. Some states provide that judgments once having become dormant may be reactivated by a motion properly brought. Once the judgment has been reinstated, the creditor may continue his efforts to effectuate collection. While most of the statutes of limitations begin to run from the date of the execution of the contract, or breach thereof, the statute on a judgment may be measured from the last affirmative action taken by the creditor towards collection.

Most statutes provide periods in which the statute is tolled. That is, there may be periods of time in which the statute does not run. Absence of the debtor from the state in which the breach of obligation occurred will normally prohibit the time period from running. Likewise, minority or incapacity will toll the statutory period.

Distinction is made in almost all states between written and oral contracts. The latter carries a shorter statute of limitations. Some states further distinguish written contracts from contracts under seal. This formality of contract is fast disappearing and is no longer of any great importance, but many states still differentiate for purposes of statutes of limitations.

TABLE B

STATUTES OF LIMITATIONS
(In Years)

STATE	Simple Contract	Sealed Instruments	Open Accounts	Promissory Notes
Alabama	6	10	3	6
Alaska	6	10	6	6
Arizona	6 written 3 oral	6	3	6
Arkansas	5 written 3 oral	5	3	5
California	4 written 2 oral	4	4	4
Colorado	6	6	6	6
Connecticut	6 written 3 oral	6	6	6
Delaware	3		3	6
Dist. of Col.	3	12	3	3
Florida	5 written 3 oral	20	3	5
Georgia	6 written 4 oral	20	4	6
Hawaii	6	6	6	6
Idaho	5 written	5	4	5

71

State	Simple Contracts	Sealed Instruments	Open Accounts	Promissory Notes
Illinois	4 oral 10 written	10	5	10
Indiana	5 oral 10 written	20	6	10
Iowa	6 oral 10 written	10	5	10
Kansas	5 oral 5 written	5	3	5
Kentucky	3 oral 15 written	15	5	15
Louisiana	5 oral usually 10		3	5
Maine	6	20	6	6
Maryland	3	12	3	3
Massachusetts	6	20	6	6
Michigan	6	6	6	6
Minnesota	6	6	6	6
Mississippi	6 written 3 oral	6	3	6
Missouri	10 written for payment of money. 5 all others.	10	5	10
Montana	8 written 5 oral	8	5	8
Nebraska	5 written 4 oral	5	4	5
Nevada	6 written 4 oral	6	4	6
New Hampshire	6	20	6	6
New Jersey	6	16	6	6
New Mexico	6 written 4 oral	6	4	6
New York	6	6	6	6
North Carolina	3	10	3	3
North Dakota	6	6	6	6
Ohio	15 written	15	6	15

STATE	Simple Contracts	Sealed Instruments	Open Accounts	Promissory Notes
Ohio	6 oral			
Oklahoma	5 written 3 oral	5	3	5
Oregon	6		6	6
Pennsylvania	6	20	6	6
Rhode Island	6	20	6	6
South Carolina	6	20	6	6
South Dakota	6	20	6	6
Tennessee	6	6	6	6
Texas	4 written 2 oral	4	2	4
Utah	6 written 4 oral	6	4	6
Vermont	6	8	6	6
Virginia	5 written 3 oral	10	3	5
Washington	6 written 3 oral	6	3	6
West Virginia	10 written 5 oral	10	5	10
Wisconsin	6	20	6	6
Wyoming	10 written 8 oral	10	6	6

The majority of states for which there is stated period of time for instruments under seal make no differentiation between simple written contracts and sealed instruments.

Statutes of Frauds

Since we have dealt with the rights of debtors and creditors under contracts, it is important to mention the various state statutes commonly referred to as the Statutes of Frauds. Basically, Statutes of Frauds requires that certain contracts be in writing to be enforceable. These types of agreements include those not to be performed within one year, a promise to pay the debt of another, a promise by an executor or administrator, a

73

promise in consideration of marriage, and the sale of goods over a fixed amount as well as the sale of any interest in real estate. We will deal here only with those contracts concerning the sale of goods in that this type of agreement most often gives rise to credit transactions.

The stated amount of the sale may vary from state to state, but because of the adoption of the Uniform Commercial Code, that amount is relatively uniform. The Uniform Commercial Code provides that contracts for the sale of goods in an amount exceeding $500 or more must be in writing to be enforceable. The contents of the contract are not specified except to the extent that it must be signed, must specify a quantity and be evidence of the agreement for the sale of goods. As between merchants, there need not be a formal contract and a written confirmation not objected to within ten days is sufficient to bind the seller.

The Statute of Frauds is an affirmative defense which must be raised by a defendant in a lawsuit before it will affect the validity of an agreement. In other words, if the seller of goods files suit on the alleged agreement claiming it to be an oral one, the defendant must answer the complaint by stating that it is unenforceable by reason of the Statute of Frauds.

Chapter VIII

EXTORTIONATE CREDIT TRANSACTIONS

A portion of the Consumer Credit Protection Act relates to an attempt by Congress to extinguish extortionate credit transactions. The legislative purpose of the Act is to do away with the credit transactions handled in such a way as to be disruptive of the bankruptcy and banking laws of the United States. These transactions are those which somehow involve force or the threat of force in making the loan or effectuating payment thereof.

Congress has determined that extortionate extension of credit, usually conducted by organized crime, can result in murder, willful injuries to person and property, and corruption of public officials. This part of the Consumer Credit Protection Act, then, is an attempt to penalize that area of organized crime which gives rise to extortionate credit.

An extortionate extension of credit in the terms of the Act is any extension of credit with respect to which it is the understanding of the creditor and the debtor at the time the extension is made, that delay in making payment or failure to make a payment could result in the use of violence. Likewise, the extension of credit would be extortionate if criminal means would be employed in the making of the obligation or in the collection of it. Criminal means include any act which would cause harm to the person, reputation or property of the debtor. Extortionate means include express threats of violence, actual violence or implied violence.

The primary features of this portion of the Act are the penalties involved for those persons convicted of extortionate credit. Any person who makes an extortionate extension of credit faces a possibility of a fine up to $10,000 and/or imprisonment for a maximum of 20 years.

A primary feature of the Act is the establishment of elements which, if proven at trial, give rise to a prima facie case of extortionate credit. If the repayment of the obligation would be unenforceable through the judicial process in a court of competent jurisdiction, the extension of credit would be prima facie extortionate if the following items were also present. The interest rate on such loan is more than 45 per cent per annum and at the time the extension of credit was made, the debtor reasonably believed that the creditor had a reputation for use of extortionate means, or the creditor had used extortionate means to collect or attempt to collect other obligations. Likewise, if the creditor had used extortionate means to punish for nonpayment of an obligation, then, with the presence of all these other elements, the loan would be deemed to have been extortionate. In order for this presumption of extortionate credit to apply, the transaction must have involved an extension of credit which, including interest, exceeded $100.

If the debtor himself is not available to testify at the trial as to what his beliefs were at the time of the extension of credit, the court may hear evidence of the creditor's reputation as to his collection practices. In a normal criminal proceeding as this is, the accused's reputation would not be at issue.

The Act further makes it a punishable offense for any person to advance money to another when the person advancing the money knows that it is to be used in an extortionate credit transaction. Actually, the person making the extension does not have to know absolutely of its purpose but rather have only reasonable grounds to believe that the money will be used in an extortionate credit transaction. Violation of this provision of the Act provides for a monetary penalty in the amount of $10,000 maximum, or an amount not exceeding twice the value of the money or property so advanced, whichever sum is the larger. A 20-year maximum jail sentence may be imposed along with the fine.

Any person who participates or conspires to use extortionate credit either in the collection or the punishment for nonpayment of such credit may face a $10,000 maximum fine or 20 years in jail, or both. In the latter situation, the reputation of the defendant creditor may be adduced in evidence, at the court's discretion.

These provisions of the Consumer Credit Protection Act, which carry with them severe penalties for violation thereof, are an attempt by Congress to eliminate extortionate credit. Of necessity, those persons who become victims of extortionate credit are those who cannot get credit through normal channels. These persons are the ones least able to afford normal rates of interest, let alone extortionate rates, and have become the victims of a highly-organized industry. The effectiveness of the extortionate credit provisions of the Act, of course, remains to be seen, but it is anticipated that it will act as a strong deterrent to the illegal practices of extortionate credit.

Chapter IX

MATHEMATICS OF CREDIT

Mention has already been made of the various factors which might affect computation of the annual percentage rate. The type of credit arrangement, of necessity, affects not only the computation of the annual percentage rate, but also the total amount of interest the debtor will have to pay. A complete mathematical explanation of interest and annual percentage rate computations would far exceed the scope of this article, but a basic understanding of these computations is important for any consumer who expects to be an aware buyer.

In cannot be reiterated too often that the basic purpose of the Consumer Credit Protection Act is to allow the consumer to shop intelligently for credit. If and when disclosures of the annual percentage rate and the total finance charges are made, the consumer may make comparisons of the costs of credit. These disclosures are, of course, to be made before consummation of the transaction, for the precise purpose of allowing comparisons of credit terms.

Even if these disclosures were not forthcoming, a consumer who understands the very basics of credit mathematics can shop for the best credit terms. One who understands the differences between simple interest, compound interest, exact interest, ordinary interest, true discount and bank discount, can at least determine if he is going to pay more or less interest on a particular transaction.

Basically, there are two types of interest computations. Simple interest is that interest computed exclusively upon the principal balance. Compound interest includes not only interest upon the principal, but also interest computed on interest. A consumer who is told that he will be paying compound interest immediately should be aware that he will be paying more than if the loan or credit extension bears simple interest.

When compound interest is computed, the basis for computation includes not only the unpaid original sum, but also any unpaid interest. Unpaid interest is added to the principal sum and the total is considered as the new principal amount for the computation of interest for the next period.

Without becoming too complicated, we should examine the basic computations of both simple and compound interest.

Simple Interest

Simple interest is computed very easily. It is merely a multiplication of the interest rate times the principal sum, times the period of time over which the loan is to be repaid. A loan of $1,000.00, at 8%, for one year requires interest payments totaling $80.00. I = $1,000 x 8% x 1 = $80.00.

The same loan for two years would cost the borrower $160.00.

Once the basic computation is understood, the variations therefrom become a bit more complicated. Simple interest can be further divided into two categories of computation: exact interest and ordinary interest. The difference between the two is the time period used in the computation. Exact interest is computed on an actual calendar year = three hundred and sixty-five days. Ordinary interest, on the other hand, is computed by using three hundred and sixty days as a full year.

The majority of simple interest computations employ the three hundred and sixty day year, but exact interest is just as acceptable.

Before setting forth some very basic interest computations, it should be understood that all interest computations are derivatives of a very simple formula or equation. That is, $I = PRT$.

In that equation the letter symbols have the following meanings:

I = the interest amount
P = the principal amount
R = the interest rate
T = the time or period over which
the loan will be outstanding

Application of this equation for a one thousand dollar loan, for a period of two years, at eight percent per annum, would be as follows:

$$I = 1,000 \times .08 \times 2$$
$$I = 160.$$

The same basic equation is, of course, used when any of the other figures are unknown. For example, if the principal amount, time and total interest are known, the rate of interest can be computed by simple rearrangement of the equation. Given the same set of loan figures used above, the computation would be as follows:

$$R = \frac{I}{PT}$$

$$R = \frac{160}{1,000} \times 2$$

$$R = \frac{160}{2,000}$$

$$R = .08 \text{ or } 8\%$$

Naturally, neither the consumer nor the creditor can be expected to manually compute each interest computation, especially when the amounts involved are large or the repayment terms become complicated. Even though the computation of simple interest, or of any of the variables which make up the equation, is relatively uncomplicated, tables are usually employed in arriving at the desired information. These compilations usually provide the exact or ordinary interest for the required number of days. For example, one such table might appear in part as follows:

Ordinary and Exact Simple Interest for $1,000 at 1%

DAYS	ORDINARY INT.	EXACT INT.
1	0.0277778	0.0272973

120	3.3333333	3.2876712
180	5.0000000	4.9315068
240	6.6666667	6.5753425
300	8.3333333	8.2191781
360	10.0000000	9.8630137

One can readily see, by examination of the above representative chart figures, that exact interest produces a slightly lower total interest figure than ordinary interest. The differential, of course, is due to the fact that ordinary interest is based upon a shorter year (360 vs. 365). This difference has been explained mathematically, and it has been determined that ordinary interest is equal to exact interest increased by 1/72 of itself. Simply stated:

$$\frac{\text{Ordinary interest}}{\text{Exact interest}} = \frac{365}{360} \text{ or } 1 + \frac{5}{360} \text{ or } 1 + \frac{1}{72}$$

These, then, are the basic types of simple interest, and their methods of computation.

Compound Interest

Although simple interest is the easiest to understand and compute, its application is not as common as is compound interest. As we already have seen, compound interest costs the borrower or credit buyer more than simple interest. The lender, or other extender of credit, of course, seeks the highest return possible on his money and, within the applicable provisions of usury laws, will normally compute interest by the method most favorable to him, subject to contractual provisions.

Compound interest can be characterized as the amount by which the original principal amount is increased over the term of the extension of credit or loan. The frequency of compounding interest will vary, depending upon the terms of the loan. This is a matter of agreement between the parties to the transaction. Interest may be compounded yearly, quarterly, monthly, or the like. The consumer should be aware that the actual rate of interest and the dollar amount of interest increases as the number of conversion intervals (compounding times) increase. In other words, a loan bearing interest at six percent. per annum, compounded monthly, would be more costly than the same loan compounded semi-annually or even quarterly.

The computation of compound interest is simple if the period of time involved is relatively short. A $1,000 loan, at 8%, compounded yearly for three years, may be figured as follows:

Original Principal Amount	$1,000.00
Interest for 1st year at 8%	80.00
New Principal	1,080.00
Interest for 2nd year	86.40
New Principal	1,166.40
Interest for 3rd year	93.31
New Principal	$1,259.71

The total interest on the above loan would be $259.71, the difference between the new principal amount at the end of the third year and the original principal. One can readily see that if the loan was for a long period of time, or if the interest was compounded more frequently than yearly, as above, the computation would become quite cumbersome. As in the case of simple interest, equations have been devised for simplifying the mathematical process.

In the following equation, these symbols are used: $S = P(1+i)^n$.

> S = the compounded amount of
>   interest and principal
> P = the original principal amount
> i = the rate of interest
> n = the number of years

This equation is appropriate only for yearly compounding. When the interest is compounded more often than once a year, the number of years (n) must be multiplied by the number of conversion intervals (m); thus mn. Likewise, the interest rate (i) must be divided by the number of conversion intervals (m); thus i/m. The letter j is often used in the equation in place of i, to indicate compound rather than simple interest. After making the appropriate changes, the equation becomes: $S = P (1 + i/m)^{mn}$.

Since it is not the intent of this chapter to delve into higher mathematics, suffice it to say that the computation of the equation requires either the use of logarithms or compound interest tables. Naturally, one who must make these computations would more readily turn to available tables than employ the use of logarithms.

A typical Compound Interest Table appears in part as follows:

Compound Amount of $1

# of Conversion Intervals	At 7% Int.	At 8% Int.
1	1.0700000	1.0800000
3	1.2254300	1.2597120
10	1.9671513	2.1589249
30	7.6122550	10.0626568
60	57.9464268	101.2570636
100	867.7163255	2199.7612563

If the table was utilized for computation of the $1,000 loan at 8% per annum for three years, the computation would be as follows:

$$S = P (1 + i)^n$$
$$S = 1,000 (1.08)^3$$

8% compounded for three periods shows on the table as 1.2597120. Thus:

$$S = 1,000 \times 1.2597120$$
$$S = \$1,259.71$$

Application of the equation along with use of the compound interest table produces the same result as the long cumbersome

83

straight mathematical computation we first applied. Of course, the same equation can be used to find any of the variables in the computation.

Instalment Sales

Simple and compound interest computations on loans are not always applicable to instalment sales situations. Basically, the method of repayment under instalment sales can take one of three forms: The payments may decrease over the term, the payments may increase, or the payments may remain constant.

When the payments are to decrease, the method of computing interest is commonly referred to as "Long-End Interest." Under that method, interest is computed on the unpaid balance of principal for the period of time between payments. Accounting for such a transaction may appear as follows:

PAYMENTS

Date	Principal	Interest	Total	Balance
Feb. 1				$ 1,000*
Feb. 1	$ 400	-	400	600
Mar. 1	200	3.00	200	400
Apr. 1	200	2.00	202	200
May 1	200	1.00	201	-0-
	$1,000	$ 6.00	$ 1,006	

Although either the "Long-End Interest" or "Short-End Interest" plan may be used in any particular transaction, as specified in the contract, the most prevalent method calls for equal payments over the instalment period. When the equal payment method is used, the total interest is computed in advance, added to the principal amount, and then divided by the number of instalment payments. Equal payment amounts are thus derived.

Any consumer who has purchased an automobile under any instalment plan has, most likely, made payments under the equal payment plan. To compute the amount of total interest one is paying under such a plan the monthly payment amount is multiplied by the number of payments. From this total the cash price

84

of the car is subtracted. The difference would be the total interest and finance charges.

Simply stated, a one-year extension of credit in the sum of $1,000, to be repaid in equal monthly instalments at 8% simple interest, will cost the consumer $80 in interest. The total amount to be repaid, then, is $1,080. This sum divided by 12 instalments results in monthly payments of $90.

Since the equal payment plan does not consider the fact that part of the principal is repaid each month, the consumer is effectively paying a higher rate of interest than 8%. Eight percent. is the nominal amount of interest, while the effective rate is much higher.

Effective Interest

As has already been pointed out, stated or nominal interest rates do not always reflect what the actual effective rate of interest is. Disclosure under the Federal Truth-in-Lending Act is an attempt to make the buyer, or borrower, aware of the real rate of interest he is paying.

There are variables which affect the computation of effective interest, but of prime concern is the conversion intervals or the number of times the nominal interest is compounded. For example: the nominal rate of 6% interest produces the following effective rates for the stated periods:

Yearly	.06
Semi-annually	.0609
Quarterly	.06136
Monthly	.06168
Weekly	.0618
Daily	.06183

The actual rate of interest may also be affected by whether or not the loan or extension of credit is discounted. As has already been mentioned, discounting also varies the annual percentage rate required to be disclosed under Truth-in-Lending.

Discounting

There are basically two types of discounting. True discount is the difference between the face value of the obligation and the present value of the debt. It can be distinguished from bank discount, which is interest deducted in advance.

A loan of $1,000 for one year at 8% simple interest would net the borrower $920 if the loan is bank discounted. Simply, the interest for the entire loan, $80, is deducted from the principal when the extension of credit is made. If, however, a true discount is applied, the result would be slightly different.

To compute a true discount the equation $S = P (1 + ni)$ is used. S = the amount to be repaid, i the interest rate, n the number of years, and P the principal at present value. Applying the same loan as above stated, the true discount method would reveal the following discount.

$$S = P (1 + ni)$$
$$P = \frac{S}{1} + ni$$
$$P = \frac{1,000}{1} + 1 \times .08$$
$$P = \frac{1,000}{1.08}$$
$$P = \$925.93$$

The true discount, then, is $1,000 minus $925.93, or $74.07 - as compared to the bank discount of $80. The true discount is, in reality, a determination of the present value of the principal amount at the stated rate of interest. Like simple and compound interest, tables are readily available for such computations.

The Present Value of 1

n	7%	8%
1	0.9345794	0.9259259
10	0.5083492	0.4631934
30	0.1313671	0.1460179
60	0.0172573	0.0098758
100	0.0011524	0.0004545

The above table shows the present value of 1 at 8% interest for one period as 0.9259259. To find the value of $1,000 the value as shown on the table is simply multiplied by 1,000, or 925.9259. Rounded to the nearest cent, we have the same answer found by application of the equation for computation of true discount - $925.93.

Consumers and borrowers should at least be aware of the method by which the interest they are to pay is computed. Basic understanding of the mathematics of finance, as it relates to interest charges, will make the consumer a wiser purchaser of credit. It cannot be stressed too often or too strongly that the purpose of Truth-in-Lending and similar legislation is to afford consumers the opportunity to shop for credit just as they shop for the best price on any item. Credit buying and credit costs constitute too large a portion of a consumer's financial life to simply buy blindly. Understanding very basic interest computations and their results will enlighten one's credit dealings.

Chapter X

CONCLUSION

The legal regulation of consumer credit has undergone considerable change during the past couple of years. The most side-sweeping changes have been effectuated by the passage of the Consumer Credit Protection Act. This Act includes the regulation of consumer credit in all its ramifications. It requires the disclosure of credit costs prior to the consummation of any consumer credit transaction. It further regulates the issuance and use of credit cards, the use of credit advertising, and the use of credit reports.

The intent and purpose of the Consumer Credit Protection Act is to make the consumer more aware of what credit actually costs him and to enhance his chances of obtaining the best credit terms when he finds it necessary to seek an extension of credit.

Before the passage of the Consumer Credit Protection Act, consumer credit was regulated by the several states in such areas as small loan acts, credit insurance, check loans and allowable interest charges. These statutes are still viable and must be understood before a consumer, and for that matter, a creditor, can intelligently enter into a credit transaction.

The substantive legal factors of a consumer credit transaction are still regulated by such enactments as the Uniform Commercial Code. Basic contract law still governs the initial agreement between a debtor and a creditor. Legislation, such as the Consumer Credit Protection Act and the proposed Uniform Consumer Credit Code, do not affect the substantive portions of a consumer credit transaction. Although a violation of the disclosure provisions of either of these Acts may take place, a debtor is not relieved from the responsibility of paying his obligation. He may be awarded damages in amounts provided by these statutes, but his obligation in contracting the debt still remains.

Every consumer must take it upon himself to familiarize himself with at least the basic aspects of the Consumer Credit Protection Act. As previously mentioned, the knowledge of the everyday consumer is highly suspect with respect to awareness of the rights and protections extended to him under the Federal legislation. Legislation is only effective if enforcement thereof is accomplished. If the consumer does not know he is to receive certain disclosure statements along with disclosures of the cost of the credit, then he will not be knowledgeable enough to prosecute actions under the Federal legislation.

Reputable dealers, financial institutions and the like, which are faced with the possibility of civil and criminal penalties under the Consumer Credit Protection Act, have taken tremendous effort to insure compliance with the Act. Even prior to its passage, courses were conducted, forms were devised, and meetings held to insure that once that Act became effective, compliance would be complete. There are going to be and there have been situations in which compliance with the Act is inadvertently omitted. In most instances, the Act recognizing the complexity of credit transactions and the vast number of transactions, has provided a method of avoiding liability for inadvertent mistakes. Absent such provisions, the courts would be swamped with alleged violations of the Consumer Credit Protection Act. The Act is intended as a shield and not a sword, in that the consumer is to be protected by the provisions and not provided with a means of obtaining financial gains. Every court hearing such actions must recognize the spirit and purpose of the legislation in determining whether or not willful violations of the Act have occurred.

It has been the intent and purpose of this Almanac to familiarize the reader with his legal rights in consumer credit transactions. No attempt has been made to set forth all of the ramifications or possible judicial interpretations of the acts, both Federal and state, which have been discussed. If a consumer believes that his rights have been violated in any consumer credit transaction, he must seek legal advice either through his own attorney or one of the many Federal or state agencies involved, to determine what his legal redress may be.

Consumers have been provided with unique and effective means of protection. It is up to each consumer effectively to use the protections granted to him.

APPENDICES

TRUTH IN LENDING

SECTION 226.3 - EXEMPTED TRANSACTIONS

This Part does not apply to the following:

(a) Business or governmental credit. Extensions of credit to organizations, including governments, or for business or commercial purposes, other than agricultural purposes.

(b) Certain transactions in security or commodities accounts. Transactions in securities or commodities accounts with a broker-dealer registered with the Securities and Exchange Commission.

(c) Non-real property credit over $25,000. Credit transactions, other than real property transactions, in which the amount financed exceeds $25,000, or in which the transaction is pursuant to an express written commitment by the creditor to extend credit in excess of $25,000.

(d) Certain public utility bills. Transactions under public utility tariffs involving services provided through pipe, wire, or other connected facilities, if the charges for such public utility services, the charges for delayed payment, and any discount allowed for early payment are filed with, reviewed by, or regulated by an agency of the Federal Government, a State, or a political sub-division thereof.

SECTION 226.6 - GENERAL DISCLOSURE REQUIREMENTS

(a) Disclosures; general rule. The disclosures required to be given by this Part shall be made clearly, conspicuously, in meaningful sequence, in accordance with the further requirements of this section, and at the time and in the terminology prescribed in applicable sessions. Where the terms "finance charge" and "annual percentage rate" are required to be used, they shall be printed more conspicuously than other terminology required by this Part. Except with respect to the requirements of 226.10, all numerical amounts and percentages shall be stated in figures and shall be printed in not less than the equivalent of 10 point type, .075 inch computer type, or elite size typewritten numerals, or shall be legibly handwritten.

SECTION 226.7 - OPEN END CREDIT ACCOUNTS - SPECIFIC DISCLOSURES

(a) Opening new account. Before the first transaction is made on any open end credit account, the creditor shall disclose to the customer in a single written statement, which the customer may retain, in terminology consistent with the requirements of paragraph (b) of this section, each of the following items, to the extent applicable:

(1) The conditions under which a finance charge may be imposed, including an explanation of the time period, if any, within which any credit extended may be paid without incurring a finance charge.

(2) The method of determining the balance upon which a finance charge may be imposed.

(3) The method of determining the amount of the finance charge, including the method of determining any minimum, fixed, check service, transaction, activity, or similar charge, which may be imposed as a finance charge.

(4) Where one or more periodic rates may be used to compute the finance charge, each such rate, the range of balances to which it is applicable, and the corresponding annual percentage rate determined by multiplying the periodic rate by the number of periods in a year.

(5) If the creditor so elects, the Comparative Index of Credit Cost in accordance with 226.11.

(6) The conditions under which any other charges may be imposed, and the method by which they will be determined.

(7) The conditions under which the creditor may retain or acquire any security interest in any property to secure the payment of any credit extended on the account, and a description or identification of the type of the interest or interests which may be so retained or acquired.

(8) The minimum periodic payment required.

SECTION 226.8 - DISCLOSURES - OTHER THAN OPEN END CREDIT

(3) The number, amount, and due dates or periods of pay-

ments scheduled to repay the indebtedness and, except in the case of a loan secured by a first lien or equivalent security interest on a dwelling made to finance the purchase of that dwelling and except in the case of a sale of a dwelling, the sum of such payments using the term "total of payments." If any payment is more than twice the amount of an otherwise regularly scheduled equal payment, the creditor shall identify the amount of such payment by the term "balloon payment" and shall state the conditions, if any, under which that payment may be refinanced if not paid when due.

(4) The amount, or method of computing the amount, of any default, delinquency, or similar charges payable in the event of late payments.

(5) A description or identification of the type of any security interest held or to be retained or acquired by the creditor in connection with the extension of credit, and a clear identification of the property to which the security interest relates or, if such property is not identifiable, an explanation of the manner in which the creditor retains or may acquire a security interest in such property which the creditor is unable to identify. In any such case where a clear identification of such property cannot properly be made on the disclosure statement due to the length of such identification, the note, other instrument evidencing the obligation, or separate disclosure statement shall contain reference to a separate pledge agreement, or a financing statement, mortgage, deed of trust, or similar document evidencing the security interest, a copy of which shall be furnished to the customer by the creditor as promptly as practicable. If after-acquired property will be subject to the security interest, or if other or future indebtedness is or may be secured by any such property, this fact shall be clearly set forth in conjunction with the description or identification of the type of security interest held, retained or acquired.

(6) A description of any penalty charge that may be imposed by the creditor or his assignee for prepayment of the principal of the obligation (such as a real estate mortgage) with an explanation of the method of computation of such penalty and the conditions under which it may be imposed.

(7) Identification of the method of computing any unearned portion of the finance charge in the event of prepayment of the

obligation and a statement of the amount or method of computation of any charge that may be deducted from the amount of any rebate of such unearned finance charge that will be credited to the obligation or refunded to the customer.

(c) Credit sales. In the case of a credit sale, in addition to the items required to be disclosed under paragraph (b) of this section, the following items, as applicable, shall be disclosed:

(1) The cash price of the property or service purchased, using the term "cash price."

(2) The amount of the downpayment itemized, as applicable, as downpayment in money, using the term "cash downpayment," downpayment in property, using the term "trade-in" and the sum, using the term "total downpayment."

(3) The difference between the amounts described in subparagraphs (1) and (2) of this paragraph, using the term "unpaid balance of cash price."

(4) All other charges, individually itemized, which are included in the amount financed but which are not part of the finance charge.

(5) The sum of the amounts determined under subparagraphs (3) and (4) of this paragraph, using the term "unpaid balance."

(6) Any amounts required to be deducted under paragraph (e) of this section using, as applicable, the terms "prepaid finance charge" and "required deposit balance," and, if both are applicable, the total of such items using the term "total prepaid finance charge and required deposit balance."

(7) The difference between the amounts determined under subparagraphs (5) and (6) of this paragraph, using the term "amount financed."

(8) Except in the case of a sale of a dwelling:

(i) The total amount of the finance charge, with description of each amount included, using the term "finance charge," and

(ii) The sum of the amounts determined under subparagraphs (1), (4), and (8)(i) of this paragraph, using the term "deferred payment price."

(d) Loans and other nonsale credit. In the case of a loan or extension of credit which is not a credit sale, in addition to the items required to be disclosed under paragraph (b) of this section, the following items, as applicable, shall be disclosed:

(1) The amount of credit, excluding items set forth in paragraph (c) of this section, which will be paid to the customer or for his account or to another person on his behalf, including all charges individually itemized, which are included in the amount of credit extended but which are not part of the finance charge, using the term "amount financed."

(2) Any amount referred to in paragraph (c) of this section required to be excluded from the amount in subparagraph (1) of this paragraph, using, as applicable, the terms "prepaid finance charge" and "required deposit balance," and if both are applicable, the total of such items using the term "total prepaid finance charge and required deposit balance."

(3) Except in the case of a loan secured by a first lien or equivalent security interest on a dwelling and made to finance the purchase of that dwelling, the total amount of the finance charge, with description of each amount included, using the term "finance charge."

(e) Finance charge payable separately or withheld; required deposit balances. The following amounts shall be disclosed and deducted in a credit sale in accordance with paragraph (c)(6) of this section, and other extensions of credit shall be excluded from the amount disclosed under paragraph (d)(1) of this section, and, shall be disclosed in accordance with paragraph (d)(2) of this section:

(1) Any finance charge paid separately, in cash or otherwise, directly or indirectly to the creditor or with the creditor's knowledge to another person, or withheld by the creditor from the proceeds of the credit extended.

(2) Any deposit balance or any investment which the creditor requires the customer to make, maintain, or increase in a specified amount or proportion as a condition to the extension of credit except:

(i) An escrow account under paragraph (e)(3) of 226.4.

(ii) A deposit balance which will be wholly applied toward satisfaction of the customers' obligation in the transaction.

(iii) A deposit balance or investment which was in existence prior to the extension of credit and which is offered by the customer as security for that extension of credit, and

(iv) A deposit balance or investment which was acquired or established from the proceeds of an extension of credit made for that purpose upon written request of the customer.

(f) <u>First lien to finance construction of dwelling</u>. In any case where a first lien or equivalent security interest in real property is retained or acquired by a creditor in connection with the financing of the initial construction of a dwelling, or in connection with a loan to satisfy that construction loan and provide permanent financing of that dwelling, whether or not the customer previously owned the land on which that dwelling is to be constructed, such security interest shall be considered a first lien against that dwelling to finance the purchase of that dwelling.

(g) <u>Orders by mail or telephone</u>. If a creditor receives a purchase order or a request for an extension of credit by mail, telephone, or written communication without personal solicitation, the disclosures required under this section may be made any time not later than the date the first payment is due, provided:

(1) In the case of credit sales, the cash price, the downpayment, the finance charge, the deferred payment price, the annual percentage rate, and the number, frequency, and amount of payments are set forth in or are determinable from the creditor's catalog or other printed material distributed to the public; or

(2) In the case of loans or other extensions of credit, the amount of the loan, the finance charge, the total scheduled payments, the number, frequency, and amount of payments, and the annual percentage rate for representative amounts of ranges of credit are set forth in or are determinable from the creditor's printed material distributed to the public, in the contract of loan, or in other printed material delivered or made available to the customer.

(h) <u>Series of sales</u>. If a credit sale is one of a series of transactions made pursuant to an agreement providing for the addition of the amount financed plus the finance charge for the current sale to an existing outstanding balance, then the disclosures required under this section for the current sale may be made at any time not later than the date the first payment for that sale is due, provided:

(1) The customer has approved in writing both the annual percentage rate or rates and the method of treating any unearned finance charge on an existing outstanding balance in computing the finance charge or charges; and

(2) The creditor retains no security interest in any property

as to which he has received payments aggregating the amount of the sale price including any finance charges attributable thereto. For the purposes of this subparagraph, in the case of items purchased on different dates, the first purchased shall be deemed first paid for, and in the case of items purchased on the same date, the lowest priced shall be deemed first paid for.

(i) <u>Advances under loan commitments</u>. If a loan is one of a series of advances made pursuant to a written agreement under which a creditor is or may be committed to extend credit to a customer up to a specified amount, and the customer has approved in writing the annual percentage rate or rates, the method of computing the finance charge or charges, and any other terms, the agreement shall be considered a single transaction, and the disclosures required under this section at the creditor's option need be made only at the time the agreement is executed.

(j) <u>Refinancing, consolidating, or increasing</u>. If any existing extension of credit is refinanced, or two or more existing extensions of credit are consolidated, or an existing obligation is increased, such transaction shall be considered a new transaction subject to the disclosure requirements of this Part. For the purpose of such disclosure, any unearned portion of the finance charge which is not credited to the existing obligation shall be added to the new finance charge and shall not be included in the new amount financed. Any increase in an existing obligation to reimburse the creditor for undertaking the customer's obligation in perfecting, protecting or preserving the security shall not be considered a new transaction subject to this Part. Any advance for agricultural purposes made under an open end real estate mortgage or similar lien shall not be considered a new transaction subject to the disclosure requirements of this section, provided:

(1) The maturity of the advance does not exceed 2 years;

(2) No increase is made in the annual percentage rate previously disclosed; and

(3) All disclosures required by this Part were made at the time the security interest was acquired by the creditor or at any time prior to the first advance made on or following the effective date of this part.

(k) <u>Assumption of an obligation</u>. Any creditor who accepts a subsequent customer as an obligor under an existing obligation shall make the disclosures required by this part to that customer before he becomes so obligated. If the obligation so assumed is secured by a first lien or equivalent security interest on a dwelling, and the assumption is made for the subsequent customer to acquire that dwelling, that obligation shall be considered a loan made to finance the purchase of that dwelling.

(l) Deferrals or extensions. In the case of an obligation other than an obligation upon which the amount of the finance charge is determined by the application of a percentage rate to the unpaid balance, if the creditor imposes a charge or fee for deferral or extension, the creditor shall disclose to the customer.

(1) The amount deferred or extended;

(2) The date to which, or the time period for which payment is deferred or extended; and

(3) The amount of the charge or fee for the deferral or extension.

(m) Series of single payment obligations. Any extension of credit involving a series of single payment obligations shall be considered a single transaction subject to the disclosure requirements of this Part.

(n) Permissible periodic statements. If a creditor transmits a periodic billing statement other than a delinquency notice, payment coupon book, or payment passbook, or a statement, billing or advice relating exclusively to amounts to be paid by the customer as escrows for payment of taxes, insurance, and water, sewer, and land rents, it shall be in a form which the customer may retain and shall set forth

(1) The annual percentage rate or rates; and

(2) The date by which, or the period, if any, within which payment must be made in order to avoid late payment or delinquency charges.

(o) Discount for prompt payment. Except as provided under 226.3(d), the amount of any discount allowed for payment of a single payment obligation on or before a specified date, or charge for delaying payment after a specified date, shall be disclosed on the billing statement as a finance charge imposed on the least amount payable in satisfaction of the obligation (amount financed) for the period of time between the specified date and the due date of the obligation, or in the absence of a designated due date, the date the billing cycle ends. Except as provided in paragraph (b)(2) of this section, each such billing statement shall, in addition to stating the amount of that "finance charge," using that term, state the "annual percentage rate," using that term, computed so that it may be disclosed with an accuracy to the near-quarter of 1 per cent and determined by (1) dividing the amount of the finance charge by the amount financed; (2) dividing the quotient so obtained by the number of days between the specified date and the due date of the obligation, or in the absence of a designated due date, the date the billing cycle cycle ends; and (3) multiplying the quotient so obtained (expressed as a percentage) by 365. (For example, a $1,000 purchase of grain, subject to terms of 2%/10 days, net 30 days, results in a "finance charge" of $20 and an amount financed $980 for a period of 20 days. The "annual percentage rate" is 37.24% which may be rounded to 37.25% or 37 1/4%).

SECTION 226.9 - RIGHT TO RESCIND CERTAIN TRANSACTIONS

(a) General rule. Except as otherwise provided in this section, in the case of any credit transaction in which a security interest is or will be retained or acquired in any real property which is used or is expected to be used as the principal residence of the customer, the customer shall have the right to rescind that transaction until midnight of the third business day following the date of consummation of that transaction or the date of delivery of the disclosures required under this section and all other material disclosures required under this Part, whichever is later, by notifying the creditor by mail, telegram, or other writing of his intention to do so. Notification by mail shall be considered given at the time mailed; notification by telegram shall be considered given at the time filed for transmission; and notification by other writing shall be considered given at the time delivered to the creditor's designated place of business.

(b) Notice of opportunity to rescind. Whenever a customer has the right to rescind a transaction under paragraph (a) of this section, the creditor shall give notice of that fact to the customer by furnishing the customer with two copies of the notice set out below, one of which may be used by the customer to cancel the transaction. Such notice shall be printed in capital and lower case letters of not less than 12 point bold-faced type on one side

101

of a separate statement which identifies the transaction to which it relates. Such statement shall also set forth the entire paragraph (d) of this section, "Effect of rescission." If such paragraph appears on the reverse side of the statement, the face of the statement shall state: "See reverse side for important information about your right of rescission." Before furnishing copies of the notice to the customer, the creditor shall complete both copies with the name of the creditor, the address of the creditor's place of business, the date of consummation of the transaction, and the date, not earlier than the third business day following the date of the transaction, by which the customer may give notice of cancellation.

SECTION 226.10 - ADVERTISING CREDIT TERMS

(a) General rule. No advertisement to aid, promote, or assist directly or indirectly any extension of credit may state

(1) That a specific amount of credit or instalment amount can be arranged unless the creditor usually and customarily arranges or will arrange credit amounts or instalments for that period and in that amount; or

(2) That no downpayment or that a specified downpayment will be accepted in connection with any extension of credit, unless the creditor usually and customarily accepts or will accept downpayments in that amount.

(b) Catalogs and multi-page advertisements. If a catalog or other multiple-page advertisement sets forth or gives information in sufficient detail to permit determination of the disclosures required by this section in a table or schedule of credit terms, such catalog or multiple-page advertisement shall be considered a single advertisement provided:

(1) The table or schedule and the disclosures made therein are set forth clearly and conspicuously, and

(2) Any statement of credit terms appearing in any place other than in that table or schedule of credit terms clearly and conspicuously refers to the page or pages on which that table or schedule appears, unless that statement discloses all of the credit terms required to be stated under this section. For the purpose of this subparagraph, cash price is not a credit term.

(c) Advertising of open end credit. No advertisement to aid, promote, or assist directly or indirectly the extension of open end credit may set forth any of the terms described in paragraph (a) of 226.7, the Comparative Index of Credit Cost, or that no downpayment, a specified downpayment, or a specified periodic payment is required or any of the following items unless it also clearly and conspicuously sets forth all the following items in terminology prescribed under paragraph (b) of 226.7:

(1) An explanation of the time period, if any, within which any credit extended may be paid without incurring a finance charge.

(2) The method of determining the balance upon which a finance charge may be imposed.

(3) The method of determining the amount of the finance charge, including the determination of any minimum, fixed, check service, transaction, activity, or similar charge, which may be imposed as a finance charge.

(4) Where one or more periodic rates may be used to compute the finance charge, each such rate, the range of balances to which it is applicable, and the corresponding annual percentage rate determined by multiplying the periodic rate by the number of periods in a year.

(5) The conditions under which any other changes may be imposed, and the method by which they will be determined.

(6) The minimum periodic payment required.

(d) Advertising of credit other than open end. No advertisement to aid, promote, or assist directly or indirectly any credit sale including the sale of residential real estate, loan, or other extension of credit, other than open end credit, subject to the provisions of this Part, shall state

(1) The rate of a finance charge unless it states the rate of that charge expressed as an "annual percentage rate," using that term;

(2) The amount of the downpayment required or that no downpayment is required, the amount of any instalment payment, the dollar amount of any finance charge, the number of instalments or the period of repayment, or that there is no charge for credit, unless it states all of the following items in terminology prescribed under 226.8:

(i) the cash price or the amount of the loan, as applicable.

(ii) the amount of the downpayment required or that no downpayment is required, as applicable.

(iii) the number, amount, and due dates or period of payments scheduled to repay the indebtedness if the credit is extended.

(iv) the amount of the finance charge expressed as an annual percentage rate. The exemptions from disclosure of an annual percentage rate permitted in paragraph (b)(2) of 226.8 shall not apply to this subdivision.

(v) Except in the case of the sale of a dwelling or a loan secured by a first lien on a dwelling to purchase that dwelling, the deferred payment price or the sum of the payments, as applicable.

RESCISSION STATEMENT

The following information is given in connection with the credit transaction

dated _____ between _____

(Seller)

and _____

(Customer)

NOTICE TO CUSTOMER REQUIRED BY FEDERAL LAW

You have entered into a transaction on _____ which may

(date)

result in a lien, mortgage, or other security interest on your home. You

have a legal right under federal law to cancel this transaction, if you desire

to do so, without any penalty or obligation within three business days from

the above date or any later date on which all material disclosures required

under the Truth in Lending Act have been given to you. If you so cancel the

transaction, any lien, mortgage, or other security interest on your home arising

from this transaction is automatically void. You are also entitled to receive a

refund of any downpayment or other consideration if you cancel. If you decide

to cancel this transaction, you may do so by notifying

_____

(Name of Creditor)

at_____

(Address of Creditor's Place of Business)

by mail or telegram sent not later than midnight of _____.

(Date)

You may also use any other form of written notice identifying the transaction if

it is delivered to the above address not later than that time. This notice may

be used for that purpose by dating and signing below.

I hereby cancel this transaction.

_____   _____

(Date)   (Customer's signature)

EFFECT OF RESCISSION. When a customer exercises his right to rescind under
paragraph (a) of this section, he is not liable for any finance or other charge,

any any security interest becomes void upon such a rescission. Within 10 days after receipt of a notice of rescission, the creditor shall return to the customer any money or property given as earnest money, downpayment, or otherwise, and shall take any action necessary or appropriate to reflect the termination of any security interest created under the transaction. If the creditor has delivered any property to the customer, the customer may retain possession of it. Upon the performance of the creditor's obligations under this section, the customer shall tender the property to the creditor, except that if return of the property in kind would be impracticable or inequitable, the customer shall tender its reasonable value. Tender shall be made at the location of the property or at the residence of the customer, at the option of the customer. If the creditor does not take possession of the property within 10 days after tender by the customer, ownership of the property vests in the customer without obligation on his part to pay for it.

DISCLOSURE STATEMENT - CREDIT CARD

When the holder of a credit card elects to use the extended payment plan, FINANCE CHARGES are applicable.

On the monthly statement sent to the cardholder, a "TOTAL FINANCE CHARGE" is shown which is the total of the amounts shown for "PERIODIC FINANCE CHARGES" and "CASH ADVANCE FINANCE CHARGES." "PERIODIC FINANCE CHARGES" are calculated on the amount of the "Previous Balance" shown on the statement, less "Payments" and "Credits" applied during the billing cycle as follows:

Periodic Rate (Monthly)	Balance to which Applicable	Annual Percentage Rate
$1\frac{1}{2}\%$	On portion up to $1,000	18%
1%	On portion over $1,000	12%

All or any part of the "New Balance" shown on your monthly statement may be paid without incurring a "PERIODIC FINANCE CHARGE" on the amount paid if payment reaches the credit service center within 25 days from the Closing Date indicated on the monthly statement.

"CASH ADVANCE FINANCE CHARGES" shown on the monthly statement are computed at $1\frac{1}{2}\%$ of the total cash advance transactions debited during the billing cycle.

MINIMUM MONTHLY PAYMENT SCHEDULE

If New Balance Is:	Minimum Payment
Under $10	Amount of New Balance
$10 to $200	$10
Over $200	5% of New Balance

Minimum payments are past due if they are not received at the credit service center within 25 days of the Closing Date indicated on the monthly statement.

DISCLOSURE STATEMENT - CREDIT SALE

lowing information is given in connection with the credit transaction

_____ between _____

(Seller)

_____

(Customer)

h Price		$_____ (1)
Cash Downpayment $_____		
Trade-In $_____ Less existing loan,		
(If any)$_____		
) Total Downpayment		$_____ (2)
paid balance of cash price (1 minus 2)		$_____ (3)
arges to be financed, itemize:		
_____ $_____		
_____		$_____ (4)
paid Balance (3 plus 4)		$_____ (5)
duct: Prepaid Finance Charge $_____		
Required Deposit Balance		
tal prepaid finance charge and required deposit balance		$_____ (6)
ount Financed (5 minus 6)		$_____ (7)
nance charge(s): $_____		
Interest $_____		
Others (itemize)		

CE CHARGE $_____ (8)

ferred Payment Price (1 plus 4 plus 8) $_____ (9)

ANNUAL PERCENTAGE RATE _____ %

ance ge Begins Accrue	Total Of Payments	Number Of Payments	Due Dates of Payments			Amount of Payments		
			First	Others	Final	First	Others	Final
	$					$	$	$

ayment charges: At the option of the seller, either 5c per $1.00 of any monthly
lment not paid within 10 days after the due date thereof (but not more than $3.00
ne defaulted installment), or 8 per cent per annum simple interest upon overdue
ts until paid.

e for prepayment, if any: $_____ or method of computing _____

```
COMPLETE ONLY IF A SEPARATE CHARGE IS MADE FOR CREDIT LIFE INSURANCE

Credit Life and Disability Insurance is not required to obtain this loan.

_____ insurance coverage is available at a cost
        (Type of Insurance)
of $_____ for the term of the credit.

I (do) (do not) desire _____ Insurance.
                          (Type or Types)

                        _____
                                (Signature)
```

This loan is secured by _____ of even date covering

(describe) _____

_____

          After acquired property   Future indebtedness is subject to or se
                                                   by the security interest.

SELLER   DATE _____

_____   BORROWER ACKNOWLEDGES RECEIPT OF A COP
                                                   THIS STATEMENT WITH APPLICABLE BLANKS
_____   COMPLETED.

By_____   _____

DISCLOSURE STATEMENT - RETAIL INSTALLMENT SALE

rs (Names & Addresses): Creditor: Loan No. _____ Date _____

_____
_____   (Street Address)
_____

_____
(City)   (State)   (Zip)

1 of ents	Finance charge	Amount financed	Annual per- centage rate	Credit life insurance charge	Disability insurance charge	Property insurance charge
$	$	$	%	$	$	$

ble in: ecutive hly allments	Due date of payments			Amount of payments			Recording fee
	First:	Others: Same day of each month	Final:	First:	Others:	Final:	
				$	$	$	$

INSURANCE

PROPERTY INSURANCE, if written in connection with this loan, may be obtained by borrower through any person of his choice. If borrower desires property insurance to be obtained through the creditor, the cost will be $_____ for the term of the credit.

CREDIT LIFE AND DISABILITY INSURANCE is not required to obtain this loan. No charge is made for credit insurance and no credit insurance is provided unless the borrower signs the appropriate statement below:

    (a) The cost for Credit Life Insurance alone will be $_____
         for the term of the credit.
    (b) The cost for Credit Life and Disability Insurance will be
         $_____ for the term of the credit.

sire Credit Life &   I desire Credit Life   I DO NOT want Credit Life
bility Insurance.   Insurance only.   or Disability Insurance.

_____   _____   _____
  Signature   Date   Signature   Date   Signature

REBATE FOR PREPAYMENT IN FULL. If the loan contract is prepaid in full by cash, a new loan, refinancing or otherwise before the final installment date, the borrower shall receive a rebate of precomputed interest computed under the Rule of 78's.

DEFAULT CHARGE. [The creditor shall set forth the amount, or method of computing the amount, of any default, delinquency, or similar charges payable in the event of late payments.]

SECURITY

Disclosure Statement - Retail Installment Sale (continued)

SECURITY

A. ( ) This loan is secured by a
security agreement of
even date covering..............

    The security agreement
will secure future or other
indebtedness and will cover
after-acquired property.

B. ( ) This loan is unsecured.

Witness: _____

	Description
( )	Motor Vehicle (s): Make: _____ Serial No: _____
( )	Household Goods & Appliances of the following description: _____
( )	Other: (Describe) _____

I acknowledge receipt of a copy of this statement

This _____ day of _____, 19___.

Borrower: _____

COGNOVIT NOTE

_____   _____, Ohio,_____, 19_____

_____after date, for value received, the undersigned jointly

 severally promise to pay to the order of _____

_____ at _____,

 sum of_____

_____Dollars, with interest from the date hereof at the rate of

_____% per annum, payable _____.

    In the event of non-payment of any principal or interest hereunder, when due,
e entire balance of principal then remaining unpaid, with accrued interest thereon,
all at once become due and payable at the option of the holder hereof, without
tice or demand.

    The maker(s) and indorser(s) hereof hereby authorize any attorney at law to
pear in any court of record of the State of Ohio or any other State in the United
ates at any time after this note becomes due, whether by acceleration or otherwise,
d to waive the issuing and service of process and confess a judgment in favor of
e legal holder hereof against the maker(s) and indorser(s), or either or any one or
re of them, for the amount of principal and interest then appearing due upon this
te, together with costs of suit and to release all errors and waive all right of
peal. If the holder hereof obtains such judgment by confession against any maker
 indorser hereof, then so long as such judgment exists, such holder, and the
ccessors and assigns thereof, hereby waive any right in respect to such judgment
 file a Certificate of Judgment for Lien, or take any other court action, if
ther would result in the acquisition of a security interest in the principal
sidence of such maker or indorser.

    The maker(s) or indorser(s) hereof hereby waive presentment, demand, notice of
ishonor, protest and notice of non-payment and protest.

    WARNING -- BY SIGNING THIS PAPER YOU GIVE UP YOUR RIGHT TO NOTICE AND COURT
RIAL. IF YOU DO NOT PAY ON TIME A COURT JUDGMENT MAY BE TAKEN AGAINST YOU WITHOUT
OUR PRIOR KNOWLEDGE AND THE POWERS OF A COURT CAN BE USED TO COLLECT FROM YOU OR
OUR EMPLOYER REGARDLESS OF ANY CLAIMS YOU MAY HAVE AGAINST THE CREDITOR WHETHER
OR RETURNED GOODS, FAULTY GOODS, FAILURE ON HIS PART TO COMPLY WITH THE AGREEMENT,
R ANY OTHER CAUSE.

ue _____   _____-

                            Residing at_____

o._____   _____

                            Residing at_____

INDEX